MARCUS GARVEY

MARCUS GARVEY
An Annotated Bibliography

COMPILED BY
LENWOOD G. DAVIS
AND
JANET L. SIMS

FOREWORD BY
JOHN HENRIK CLARKE

GREENWOOD PRESS
WESTPORT, CONNECTICUT • LONDON, ENGLAND

Library of Congress Cataloging in Publication Data

Davis, Lenwood G
Marcus Garvey : an annotated bibliography.

Includes index.
1. Garvey, Marcus, 1887-1940—Bibliography.
I. Sims, Janet L., 1945- joint author.
Z8324.49.D38 [E185.97.G3] 016.3058'96'024 80-653
ISBN 0-313-22131-6 (lib. bdg.)

Library of Congress Catalog Card Number: 80-653
ISBN: 0-313-22131-6

First published in 1980

Greenwood Press
A division of Congressional Information Service, Inc.
88 Post Road West, Westport, Connecticut 06881

Printed in the United States of America

10 9 8 7 6 5 4 3 2 1

Dedicated to
Black People Everywhere

Contents

Foreword

This annotated bibliography is both timely and long overdue. It complements the new interest in Marcus Garvey and his organization, the Universal Negro Improvement Association (UNIA) that was started with the publication of E. David Cronon's book, *Black Moses, The Story of Marcus Garvey and the Universal Negro Improvement Association* (1955). This interest was continued with the book *Garvey and Garveyism* by his widow, Amy Jacques Garvey, that was published privately by Mrs. Garvey in Jamaica in 1962 and reprinted in the United States in 1970. General interest in Marcus Garvey declined after his death in 1940; however, a number of master theses and doctoral dissertations were written about Marcus Garvey and the rise and fall of the UNIA, the largest Black Mass Movement that has ever been developed outside of Africa.

More than anyone else, Amy Jacques Garvey is responsible for keeping the legacy of Marcus Garvey alive. The foundation for this legacy is the collection of his early speeches, *Philosophy and Opinions of Marcus Garvey*, first published in 1923. The Civil Rights Movement and its aftermath, the debate over Black Nationalism, and the African Independence Explosion renewed interest in Marcus Garvey and his thinking in the 1960s. A rash of new books, both good and bad, followed this resurgence of interest. In my opinion, the best of the recent books on Marcus Garvey is *Race First*, by Professor Tony Martin. Dr. Martin examines some of the neglected dimensions of Marcus Garvey.

In the opening statement of his book Dr. Martin moves beyond so much of the early works on Marcus Garvey when he states:

> This book is based on the simple premise that no one could have organized and built up the largest Black mass movement in Afro-American History, in the face of con-

tinuous onslaughts from Communists on the left, black reactionaries on all sides, and the most powerful governments in the world, and yet be a buffoon or a clown, or even an overwhelmingly impractical visionary.

This is where we need to begin a reexamination of the impact of Marcus Garvey on his time and his people. He is probably one of the most misunderstood men in the history of African people. In referring to Garvey, Tony Martin says: "Distortions are not new to Afro-American history, but one would be hard put to find a major Black figure who has suffered more at the hands of historians and commentators."

Now that Africa is in the last phase of the long fight for liberation, it is time to take a more serious look at Marcus Garvey, who, more than any other organization leader, made Western Blacks aware of Africa as their motherland. It is time, Professor Martin maintains, to "examine the major features of Garvey's ideological outlook, as they manifested themselves both in theory and in practice."

The rise and fall of Marcus Garvey is one of the great epics in twentieth-century Black history. Both he and his movement stubbornly refused to disappear after their days of triumph were over.

It is no accident that Marcus Garvey had his greatest success among Blacks in the United States. There is a historical logic to this success that is rooted in the nature of the oppression of Black people in America. Psychologically, American oppression makes the deepest wound and leaves the longest scar. Marcus Garvey came to the United States and began to build his movement at a time of great disenchantment among Afro-Americans, who had pursued the "American Dream" until they had to concede that the dream was not dreamed for them. They had listened to the "American Promise" and conceded that the promise was not made to them. These realizations only complicated their lives, because they could not disassociate themselves from the American Dream and the American Promise. Nothing else gave American Blacks the vision of a new dream, a new promise, and a new land.

Garvey was an experienced leader before he came to the United States. He came out of a radical leadership tradition, and was a strike leader before he was twenty years old. In 1910, he made his first trip abroad and became concerned with working conditions among Caribbean laborers in Costa Rica and other parts of Central America. In 1912, he made his first trip to London. Here he saw new dimensions of the Blacks' struggle and was exposed to ideas that would help formulate his life's work. His relationship with Duse Mohammed Ali, an Egyptian nationalist of Sudanese descent, helped to shape his ideas about African redemption. He had come to the administrative headquarters of the British Empire to acquaint himself with the realities of dealing with massive powers.

A year before Marcus Garvey arrived in London, the city had been host to a World Congress on Race (July 1911). The literature, the attitudes, and the debates about the Congress were still prevailing when Marcus Garvey began his London years.

In July 1914, he returned to Jamaica with ideas for a new organization, the Universal Negro Improvement and Conservation Association and African Communities League. This was the beginning of the dream that he would try to make into a reality.

Marcus Garvey came to the United States in 1916, convinced that he had been called upon "to emancipate his race." Thus began his years of triumph and tragedy.

He was no stranger to conditions in the United States. His wide reading on racial matters had introduced him to the conflicts and contradictions in Black-American life. He arrived in the United States in the midst of two large-scale migrations of Blacks: one from the West Indies and another from the American South. The main constituents of the UNIA during its formative years were drawn from these two migrations.

Between 1920 and 1925, the Garvey Movement rose to great heights and, in spite of its troubles, continued to grow. In this period the movement had its greatest success and was under the severest criticism. The convention of 1920 was a monumental achievement in Black organizations. The convention came in the years after the First World War when the promises to Black Americans had been broken, lynchings were rampant, and Blacks were still recovering from "the Red Summer of 1919," in which there were race riots in most of the major American cities. During this time Garvey brought the Black Star Line into being and into a multiplicity of troubles.

Marcus Garvey's Race First and Self-Reliance Program became known, and in most cases respected, throughout the African World. He attracted to his ranks some of the major Black writers and thinkers of his day. Conversely, some of the same group were his severest critics.

Writers such as Claude McKay, Eric Walrond, and Zora Neale Hurston wrote for the UNIA paper *Negro World* at various times during its existence. William H. Ferris and Hubert H. Harrison, more radical thinkers, contributed penetrating book reviews and articles to *Negro World*. Garvey's personality and the movement he founded, together with the writers and artists of the Renaissance Period, helped to put Harlem on the map. While the literary aspect of the Renaissance was unfolding, Marcus Garvey and his Universal Negro Improvement Association, using Harlem as a base of operation, built the largest mass movement among Black people that this country had ever seen. This movement had international importance and was considered to be a threat to the colonial powers of Europe that were entrenched in Africa.

For about twelve years, Harlem was Marcus Garvey's window to the world. From this vantage point, he became a figure of international importance. This magnetic and compelling personality succeeded in building a mass movement after other men had failed, perhaps because he lived in an age of conflict that affected African peoples everywhere.

The appearance of the Garvey Movement was perfectly timed. The broken promises of the postwar period had produced widespread cynicism in the Black population that had lost some of its belief in itself as a people. Adam Clayton Powell, Sr., wrote of Garvey: "He is the only man that ever made Negroes who are not Black ashamed of their color." In his book, *Marching Blacks*, Adam Clayton Powell, Jr., wrote: "Marcus Garvey was one of the greatest mass leaders of all time. He was misunderstood and maligned, but he brought to the Negro people, for the first time, a sense of pride in being Black."

The Garvey Movement had a profound effect on the political development of Harlem and on the lives of both the Adam Clayton Powells. The fight to make Harlem a congressional district began during the Garvey Period.

Garvey and his movement had a short and spectacular life span in the United States. His movement took effective form in about 1919, but in 1926 he was in a federal prison, charged with misusing the mails. From prison he was deported home to Jamaica. This is the essence of the Garvey saga in America.

Marcus Garvey, who was elected Provisional President of Africa by his followers, was never allowed to set foot on African soil. He spoke no African language. But Garvey managed to convey to African people everywhere, and to the rest of the world, his passionate belief that Africa was the home of a civilization that had once been great and would be great again. When one considers the slenderness of Garvey's resources and the vast material forces, social conceptions, and imperial interests that sought to destroy him, his achievement becomes one of the great propaganda miracles of this century.

Garvey's voice reverberated inside Africa itself. The King of Swaziland told Mrs. Marcus Garvey that he knew the names of only two Black men in the Western world: Jack Johnson, the boxer who defeated a White man, Jim Jeffries, and Marcus Garvey.

In this book, *Marcus Garvey: An Annotated Bibliography*, Dr. Lenwood G. Davis, historian, biographer, author, compiler, editor, and noted bibliographer, and Ms. Janet L. Sims, librarian, bibliographer, compiler, and writer, have carefully compiled lists of the most relevant materials relating to Marcus Garvey and the movement that he spearheaded. This book will facilitate the study of Marcus Garvey and Black movements in the twentieth century and will be thought-provoking, enlightening, and compelling to everyone interested in Marcus Garvey and Garveyism.

JOHN HENRIK CLARKE
Professor of African History
Hunter College, New York City

Introduction

Although Marcus Garvey's critics called him a "lunatic," "mad man," "clown," "fraud," "jackass," "buffoon," "monkey," and a "dupe," all agreed that he organized the largest mass movement of Black people in the United States. Many people see his movement primarily as being a "Back-to-Africa" movement. That concept is erroneous. His movement was broader and more comprehensive than that: he advocated total redemption for the African continent. Garvey also stressed social, political, and economic uplift, and racial pride on the part of Blacks in the United States, West Indies, and Africa. He saw and understood the need for unity among Black people worldwide.

Marcus Garvey arrived on the American scene at the right time. The death of Booker T. Washington caused a void in Black leadership in the United States. Blacks in America were disillusioned with society and believed conditions were not improving for them. They saw a resurgence of the Ku Klux Klan, continuation of lynching of Blacks, and a government too passive to protect them from these and other atrocities.

After Blacks fought and died in World War I, they thought they would finally share in the "American Dream" and reap some of its rewards. This illusion was soon shattered with the "Red Summer" race riots of 1919. Furthermore, they lost previously-won gains when newly-elected President Woodrow Wilson reinstated segregation in federal facilities. Garvey pointed out to Black people in the United States that as long as they stayed in this country, they would not find justice and equality. They had only one alternative: to leave this racist country and emigrate to Africa, their ancestral home.

To carry out his vision, Garvey organized the Universal Negro Improvement Association (UNIA). This organization first had its headquarters in

Jamaica but later moved to New York City where it could be more visible and gain more support.

In 1920 the UNIA held its first International Convention of the Negro Peoples of the World in New York City at Madison Square Garden. More than 25,000 people attended this month-long meeting and heard Garvey proclaim, "Africa for the Africans, those at home and those abroad." Perhaps the most positive thing to come out of this monumental meeting was a document entitled, "The Declaration of The Rights of The Negro Peoples of the World."

The Garvey Movement reached its zenith between 1920 and 1925. During this time Garvey attracted millions of followers and raised millions of dollars. Marcus Garvey's name became a household word for many Blacks. He bought the Black Star Line shipping company and founded the African Orthodox Church in the United States. Garvey also established many Black owned and operated businesses, including the Negro Factories Corporation that assisted Black businesses.

The Garvey Movement virtually collapsed in 1923 when Garvey was indicted by the United States government for using the U.S. mail to sell allegedly fraudulent stocks in the Black Star Line. It is apparent from the court records that Garvey's subordinates defrauded people, although he himself had no intentions of exploiting his supporters. Nevertheless, Garvey was sentenced in 1925 to five years in the federal penitentiary in Atlanta, Georgia. After serving two years he was pardoned and deported to his native country, Jamaica, as an "undesirable alien."

While in Jamaica, he continued to reorganize his movement and redefine its goals. In 1934, he moved the headquarters of UNIA to London in hope of gaining more support. Because of the two-year depression in the United States, the lack of financial support from Black Americans, and the loss of millions of followers, the Garvey Movement became ineffective, and would never again reach the prominence that it once had. Marcus Garvey died in England on June 10, 1940, without having seen his dream fulfilled. Neither he nor any of his followers emigrated to Africa.

This bibliography is timely because of the revival of Garveyism and the "Africa for the Africans" movement, especially in the southern part of the African continent. There is evidence to support the supposition that Garvey was the forerunner of the "Black Is Beautiful" concept and the Black Power movement in the United States.

This work includes many of the speeches and writings of Garvey from his organization (UNIA) and its two newspapers, *Negro World* and *Black Man*. Garvey also wrote a number of poems that appear in these newspapers. There are also his own books, including *The Philosophy and Opinions of Marcus Garvey*. In addition to these works, there is his wife's work, Amy Jacques Garvey's *Garvey and Garveyism*. Also included in this work are the leading Black newspapers and periodicals of that time that carried extensive coverage of him. The major Black newspapers include: *The New York Age, The Norfolk Journal and Guide, New York Amsterdam News*, and *The Pittsburgh Courier.* The major periodicals consist of *Crisis, Opportunity*, and *The Messenger.*

While there are unpublished materials on Marcus Garvey, this bibliography deals only with published materials. The reason for limiting this work is our objective to expose the layman, general public, and researcher to the voluminous amount of published materials on Garvey that is easily accessible to them.

There are, however, two institutions that have a large amount of unpublished materials on Garvey—Fisk University in Nashville, Tenn. and the Schomburg Research Center in New York City. The private papers of Amy Jacques Garvey and the FBI file on Marcus Garvey and other papers are at Fisk University. There are many items there that are not well known. The Schomburg Collection has a large body of Garvey materials that was found in an abandoned house. This material is now available to scholars.

Several individuals have amassed large collections of materials on Garvey. Professor Robert Hill, at the Afro-American Studies Program at the University of California at Los Angeles, has assembled the largest body of Garvey material in the United States. He is presently preparing eleven volumes of the *Papers of Marcus Garvey and the UNIA: 1910–1940*, to be published by the University of California Press. John Henrik Clarke, Professor of History in the Department of Black and Puerto Rican Studies at Hunter College has a number of extensive taped interviews of Mrs. Garvey speaking about her husband and additional materials on the leader. Bernice Simms of New York City has some UNIA papers dating from 1918 to 1959. Others have collected substantial amounts of material while working on their doctoral dissertations: Tony Martin, Randall K. Burkett, Shirley Wilson Strickland, Emory Joel Tolbert, and Shirley Nash Webser.

This bibliography is divided into eight parts. Part One lists books by Marcus Garvey. Part Two includes selected articles by Garvey. Part Three consists of major books on the leader. Part Four includes general books. We included significant sections of books that discuss Garvey and those that give a different or unique slant on the subject. Part Five includes major articles. We consider major articles as those having four or more pages and authors who wrote two or more articles included herein. Part Six deals with general articles from newspapers, magazines, journals, and periodicals and represents the largest section in this work. Part Seven includes dissertations and theses. Part Eight is the "Constitution and Book of Laws of the Universal Negro Improvement Association and African Communities' League." An extensive index rounds out the work.

This bibliography, like any bibliography, has as its main shortcoming the omission of certain works. We are assured that some will want to know why we did not include certain materials. There are two reasons: first, we included only those works that we personally read and annotated, and second, we were unaware of the existence of certain works and of their availability to us. In spite of the shortcomings of this work, we feel that this annotated bibliography is the most comprehensive and exhaustive compiled to date on Marcus Garvey. We welcome any corrections or additions, since we hope to update this work at a later date.

1

BOOKS BY MARCUS GARVEY

---

1. A Talk with Afro-West Indians: The Negro Race and Its Problems. Kingston: African Communities League, 1915.

   The writer discussed the history of West Indians. He points out that West Indians did not do all they could to gain their independence from the European colonizers. Garvey also declared that Black people should know their own history.

2. Conspiracy of the East Saint Louis Riots. NY: UNIA, 1917.

   This short pamphlet by the leader denounced the riots in East St. Louis.

3. Eight Uncle Tom Negroes and W. E. Burghardt DuBois As A Hater of Dark People. NY: Press of the UNIA, 1923.

   The title depicts what this work is about. Much of this work deals with Dr. DuBois. The leader asserts that DuBois "Calls His Own Race 'Black And Ugly,' Judging From The White Man's Standard of Beauty."

4. Aims and Objects of Movement for Solution of Negro Problem Outlined, Asks White Race to be Considerate and Symphathetic, Help Negroes to Have A Nation of Their Own in Africa, Friendly Appeal of Negro for His Race. NY: Universal Negro Improvement Association, 1924.

   The title tells what this short nine page pamphlet discusses. The following topics are included: "The Spiritual Brotherhood of Man," "Supplying a Long Felt Wand," "Should Not Legalize Mongrelization of Races," "Liberal Whites and Race Loving Negroes," "The Ambition of Negroes Who Seek Social Equality," "Relationship of Negroes to Each Other," "Claims of Africa," "Help the Negro to Return Home," and "Lazy Negroes Who Prefer East to Labor." The writer concluded by declaring "The Universal Negro Improvement Association is composed of all shades of Negroes - Black, Mulattoes, and Yellows, who are working honestly for the purification of their races, and for a symphathetic adjustment of the race problem."

5. Selections from the Poetic Meditations of Marcus Garvey. Edited by Amy Jacques Garvey, NY: n.p., 1927.

A collection of poems written by the leader. A number of them were written when he was in prison in Atlanta, take up the argument against fatalism. They include: "Why Disconsolate,?" "Have Faith in Self," and "Find Yourself."

6. The Tragedy of White Injustice. NY: A. J. Garvey, 1927.

A collection of poems by the leaders. Many of his poems dealt with liberation. The leader also wrote about Black women, Africa, Italians,and Ethopia.

7. Speech at Royal Albert Hall - London, England: The Case of The Negro for International Racial Adjustment. London: Universal Negro Improvement Association, 1928.

This is a major speech made in London and Garvey presented to the English people the claim of the Black Race upon their civilization. He traces the history of European interest in Africa including the slavery trade in Africa and America. The leader told the audience that Blacks love their race not for social fellowship but in the common brotherhood that God intended we should live. Garvey concludes that we (Blacks) are only going to ask you to give us (Blacks) a fair chance, a fair opportunity to express ourselves (Black people) in terms of reason.

8. Minutes of Proceedings of the Speech by the Honorable Marcus Garvey at the Century Theater. London: Vail Co., 1928.

The leader's responses to historian H. G. Wells concerning the history of the Black man. He argues that the Blacks know that they have a history and that they are proud of their past. Garvey concludes that he would be nothing else in God's creation but a Black man.

9. Universal Negro Improvement Association Convention Hymns. Kingston: 1934.

This title tells what this book is about. Many of these hymns were composed by the leader and are of a political nature. Others were of a religious nature.

10. A Grand Speech of Honorable Marcus Garvey at Kingsway Hall, London Denouncing the Moving Picture Propaganda to Discredit the Negro. London: Black Man Publishing Co., 1939.

The title explains what this book is about. The leader devotes a great deal of time denouncing Paul Robeson, the leading Black actor of that period. He argues that Robeson's roles demeaned Black people.

2
ARTICLES BY MARCUS GARVEY

11. "West Indies In The Mirror Of Truth." Champion Magazine, January, 1917, p. 267.

The leader declared that a Frederick Douglass or a Booker T. Washington never would have been heard of in American national life if it were not for the consciousness of the race in having its own leaders. He concludes that the West Indies has produced no such leaders as Douglass and Washington, after 78 years of emancipation, simply because the Negro people of that section started out without a race consciousness.

12. "The Negroes' Greatest Enemy." Current History, Vol. 18, September, 1923, pp. 951 - 957.

This article, which is largely autobiographical, discusses Garvey's background, his ideals, and the implementation of those ideals, and the impact of the Universal Negro Improvement Association. Garvey also focused on the future struggle of Blacks.

13. "Speech Before Incarceration in The Tombs Prison, June 17, 1923," in John Henrik Clarke, Marcus Garvey and The Vision of Africa. NY: Vintage Books, 1974, pp. 150 - 151.

The leader states he has entered the fight for the emancipation of race; Marcus Garvey has entered the fight for the redemption of a country. He concludes that the world is crazy and foolish if they think that they can destroy the principles, and ideals of the Universal Negro Improvement Association.

14. "An Apostrophe to Ms. Nancy Cunard." New Jamaican, July 28, 1932.

The writer contends that the world wonders why Ms. Nancy Cunard thinks symphathetically Black. It is with the same reason that the Black man thinks symphathetically White whenever any outrage is attempted or perpetrated upon White race anywhere. He concludes that when Ms. Cunard is gone the way of physical beings, her kindly thoughts, her gentle mental symphathies for a race downtrodden and oppressed shall live forever.

15. "Letter to Guy M. Walker," in John Henrik Clarke, Marcus Garvey and The Vision of Africa. NY: Vintage Books, 1974, 152 - 155.

This was a letter written by the leader to Guy M. Walker. The author asked Mr. Walker to answer eleven questions so that he might be able to judge how much symphathy there is among the leaders of the White race in this country. Some of the questions include: Do you believe the Negro to be a human being? Do you believe that the Negroes should have a government of their own in Africa?

16. "The World As It Is." The Black Man, December, 1933, Vol. 1, No. 1, pp. 2 - 5.

The writer discusses Adolph Hitler, the dollar flops, dual cultures, George S. Schuyler, and Communism, and the Negro. He contends that it would be very unwise for Blacks to encourage one as pronounced in his views as Hitler. Hats off to Hitler the German Nazi, and hats off to the new spirit of the Negro that will challenge not only Hitler, but any political leader who would dare intrude upon the rights of Africa. Garvey argues that the English and French, in a skillful combination, have checked the American march in finance, and so the dollar goes down. He states that the United States is still the land of dual cultures - that of a highly developed civilization and that of barbarism. The leader declares that George S. Schuyler was one of the most dangerous libelers of true American Negro character and has done more harm to the cause of the American Negro that most of the enemies of that race we know. The author concludes that Communism is trying to change the political systems of the world and it is not fair that the Negro should be sacrificed at the early stages of the battle for the benefit of those who will come after in the centuries.

17. "What Is The UNIA?" The Black Man, December, 1933, No. 1, pp. 5 - 7.

The writer discusses the history of the organization since its inception in 1914 in Jamaica to 1933.

He contends that this organization reaches into the fundamentals of all that is humanly worthy in a people. He concludes that the program of the UNIA is so concrete that it cannot be improved upon.

18. "The Negro and Himself." The Black Man, December, 1933, Vol. 1, No. 1, pp. 12 - 14.

Garvey states that the great battles that have been fought against the UNIA for its elimination and destruction were chiefly conducted by Negroes themselves, on behalf of the other races that seek the permanent subjugation of the Black Man. He concludes that: "No one can destroy the Negro but himself."

19. "Marcus Garvey Declares Himself." The Black Man, December 1920, Vol. 1, No. 1, pp. 19 - 20.

Garvey mentions in this open letter to fellowmen of the Negro Race that he experienced great surprise at the fraudulent misrepresentations undertaken in his name, to misrepresent and deceive Black people concerning his activities. He argues that Blacks must have proper organization to fight their oppressors. The leader appealed to Blacks for financial support to carry out his work.

20. "Roosevelt's Task." The Black Man, January, 1934, Vol. 1, No. 2, pp. 3 - 5.

He states that Franklin D. Roosevelt is today the most important leader of democracy. Garvey sees as his greatest enemy and enemy of the American people, the financiers, bankers, and gambling speculators who have, for decades, under the patronage of the Republican Party, built up an unholly sovereignty in finance that has deprived the average American citizen of his just economic dues. The leader concludes that the Negro should rally around Roosevelt and the Democratic Party.

21. "An Appeal to the American Negro!" The Black Man, January, 1934, Vol. 1, No. 2, pp. 8 - 11.

Garvey surmises that whether American Negroes continue to accept him for any length of time as their leader or not, it is their duty to always be sober and sane in their judgments and in their acts.

22. "The World As It Is." The Black Man, January, 1934, Vol. 1, No. 2, pp. 12 - 14.

Garvey points out that the mismanagement of Newfoundland shows that the Negro is not the only one who is unable to manage his own national affairs. It was mentioned that the government of Liberia had scores of political prisoners locked in jails because they oppose the slave traffic in Liberia. He also gives the reasons for the fall of the American dollar.

23. "God's Chosen People?" The Black Man, January, 1934, Vol. 1, No. 2, pp. 17 - 18.

The writer argues that God's Chosen People are discussed in the Bible in the story of Revelation. He concludes that Revelations gives the chart to every man and Negroes should study carefully the words of Revelation. On them will hinge, by the acceptance of the truth therein, the Divine hope of the Negro.

24. "Garvey's Urge to Greater Organization." January, 1934, Vol. 1, No. 2., pp. 19 - 20.

In a letter to his fellowmen of the Negro Race, he calls upon the populace everywhere to forget the narrow bounds of selfish community or national life and assume the responsibility of the greater urge toward a united front that will make us comrades in the grand and glorious fight for universal liberty.

25. "America and the Negro." The Black Man, February, 1934, Vol. 1, No. 3, pp. 1 - 3.

Garvey believes that if the Negro, as an American citizen, makes a concentrated fight for his civil rights, he will not only force America to hear him, but will also force the world into recognizing the justice of his pleas; and world opinions, when properly aroused, is never slow to express itself on behalf of the injured.

26. "A Message to Members of the UNIA and Allied Organizations." The Black Man, February, 1934, Vol. 1, No. 3, pp. 3 - 5.

Garvey states that Negroes must eliminate their jealousies, their hatred, their dislikes for and against each other, remembering that if they are to be a united race, every unit of the race must be in harmony with the UNIA.

27. "The Urge Has Come." The Black Man, February, 1934, Vol. 1, No. 3, pp. 6 - 7.

In this letter to his fellowmen of the Negro Race, Garvey urged all Negroes to unite now to fight their enemies all over the world that are oppressing Black people. He states that Negroes should not fight oppressors outside of the UNIA, but inside it, by supporting it financially.

28. "The American Government and the Negro." The Black Man, February, 1934, Vol. 1, No. 3, pp. 7 - 8.

Garvey asserts that Roosevelt's Government must be given a chance to play fair with the Negro. The Negro can be a great and useful asset to America as part of its constitutional body. He concludes that the Negro is not Communistic, he is not rebellious, and the American nation can be dependent upon him always to do the right thing, if he is treated fairly.

29. "The World As It Is." The Black Man, February, 1934, Vol. 1, No. 3, pp. 9 - 12.

Garvey calls George S. Schuyler a monkey and not a true journalist. He called Charles A. Lindbergh a wonderful American and a credit to the White race. The writer argues that the Negro Race wants characters like Lindbergh who will not only soar above in an airplane, but who will soar above even in nearly every walk of life.

30. "Wake Up Black Men!" The Black Man, February, 1934, Vol. 1, No. 3, pp. 15 - 16.

Garvey states that Negroes must occupy their own time doing the things that are worthwhile in science, art, literature, engineering, statesmanship, industry, commerce, nation-building, and in empire expansion. He urged Negroes to get busy and build up their civilization.

31. "A Thoughtful Man." The Black Man, March - April, 1934, Vol. 1, No. 4, pp. 1 - 2.

Garvey states that President Roosevelt of the United States is showing himself as a very thoughtful statesman, whose prejudices, if any, are at a minimum as far as the question of races goes. Since his occupancy of The White House as the Chief Executive of the American nation, he has been doing much to advance the political and social interests of Negro Americans.

32. "Adolph Hitler." The Black Man, March - April, 1934, Vol. 1, No. 4, pp. 2 - 3.

Garvey argues that Africa affords a greater opportunity for a Hitler than anywhere else among Negroes because the appeal could easily be made on nationalistic bases. He concludes that he hoped sooner or later that the Negro would find his plans and produce his Hitler.

33. "Find Your Work!" The Black Man, March - April, 1934, Vol. 1, No. 4, pp. 3 - 5.

Garvey urges Negroes to become self-employed.

He points out that Negroes have slept too long and remained idle too long. The leader concludes that Negroes must be moving onward and upward, both mentally and physically.

34. "Is America Hell?" The Black Man, March - April, 1934, Vol. 1, No. 4, p. 6.

The writer contends that the Southern section of the United States has no rivals in barbarism. He concludes that if America fails to take on the vision of love, and humanity, and she perishes, it will be her own fault.

35. "The World As It Is." The Black Man, March - April, 1934, Vol. 1, No. 4, pp. 9 - 10.

The leader states that George S. Schuyler is a dangerous Negro to the American people because he has attacked and mercilessly libeled nearly every honest Negro and Negro Movement, seeking to do good for the race in America. He contends that the Negro civilization is really an adaptation of the glories and achievements of men and women who have blazed trails in different departments of humanity. He concludes that the American Negro has become a creator in art.

36. "A Drifting Race." The Black Man, March - April, 1934, Vol. 1, No. 4, p. 11.

Garvey argues that he does not promise the Negro anything more phenomenal than his own willingness to intelligently cooperate to solve his own problems. He states that the UNIA offers a practical hope to the Negro people of the world.

37. "The Negro As Colonizer." The Black Man, March - April, 1934, Vol. 1, No. 4, pp. 15 - 16.

The leader feels that the only Negroes that were successful colonists were of the West Indies in Haiti under Toussant L'Overture. If colonization with the ultimate object of nationalization is good for the White man, it is also good for the Black Man. He concludes that the American Negro, the West Indian Negro, and all Negroes of the Western Hemisphere should now think seriously about the proper schemes of colonization.

38. "Dr. DuBois Criticized." The Black Man, May - June, 1934, Vol. 1, No. 5, pp. 1 - 2.

Garvey calls DuBois a vain opportunist who held onto the honors and glory showered upon him because he was one of the first experiments of higher Negro education. He states that DuBois was never born a leader and has none of the leadership qualities. He concludes that the Negro should not deprive himself nor the world of that which is particularly his, and so it is advisable that all units of the race concentrate upon the great idea of cultural imperialism.

39. "The Negro and Character." The Black Man, May - June, 1934, Vol. 1, No. 5, pp. 5 - 6.

The writer surmises that it is unfortunate that the Negro has not yet developed a proper racial code, one that can be adhered to by each political unit, and each individual. He surmises that whatsoever may be, Black codes to a race, the most outstanding principle of it should be the development of good character.

40. "Negro Psychology." The Black Man, May - June, 1934, Vol. 1, No. 5, pp. 7 - 8, 14.

Garvey contends that the difference of races is purely a difference of character and outlook and that the Negro civilizations have not yet reached their zenith. He concludes that the Negro must develop courage, character, and will and do with these traits what he can to rise above men as the sun rises to reach the highest point at mid-day.

41. "The World As It Is." The Black Man, May - June, 1934, Vol. 1, No. 5, pp. 9 - 10.

The editor declares that the Americans ought to adopt some of the English methods of free speech and by maintaining good government they would have no need to be afraid of any new thing. It would be better for America to let those who have new ideas speak them out in public than to have them organize ideas in private or secretly.

42. "Centennary of Negro Emancipation." The Black Man, May - June, 1934, Vol. 1, No. 5, pp. 11 - 12.

The writer states that because the West Indian Negroes were freed in 1834, it is considered that this is the proper year to celebrate the Centennary of Emancipation. He concludes that when the American and West Indian Negroes get to know their histories, there will nationally spring up among them a better feeling of symphathy and comradeship, and when both of them become more conscious of their own origins, they will have a greater love for the African, through whom they have been sired.

43. "An Advice and Statement." The Black Man, May - June, 1934, Vol. 1, No. 5, p. 12.

The leader declares that some individuals are misrepresenting both he and the UNIA in the United States.

He states that neither he nor the UNIA will be destroyed by misrepresentations of rogues and vagabonds.

44. "The Negro Race." The Black Man, May - June, 1934, Vol. 1, No. 5, pp. 15 - 16.

The editor argues that as much as the White man may boast of his glorious deeds today, the fact remains that what he now knows was inherited from the original minds of the Black Men who made Egypt, Carthage, and Babylon, the centers of Civilization, that were not known to the unskilled and savage men of Europe. He concludes that the greatest accomplishments of humanity are very possible to the Negro today, because they were in ages past!!!

45. "The West Indian Negro." The Black Man, May - June, 1934, Vol. 1, No. 5, pp. 17 - 18.

The leader contends that the greatest misfortune surrounding the West Indian Negro at home is his inability to develop a true racial consciousness in the midst of an environment that would make him master of the situation. He concludes that if the West Indian Negro thinks and does so deeply, even though he is circumvented by peculiar laws, he can rise above them to the advantage of himself, by being a real man.

46. "The Call to A Purposeful Life." The Black Man, May - June, 1934, Vol. 1, No. 5, pp. 19 - 20.

In the letter to his fellowmen of the Negro Race, the leader points out that the sons and daughters of Africa, and the Africans at home, must fall in line with the UNIA and make us, one and all, devotees of the cause of racial life, racial love, leading to racial triumph and racial glory.

47. "Marcus Garvey Opens International Convention With Great Speech." The Black Man, November, 1934, Vol. 1, No. 6, pp. 4 - 12.

Garvey delivered this speech at the Seventh International Convention of the Negro Peoples of the World, held in London, England. The leader espoused a number of topics: the problems of Black people, intelligence of convention members, revealed the facts about present day American Negroes, conditions in Britain relative to Negroes, the sins of men, Christianity, the blessings of God, and proper leadership.

48. "The Outlook." The Black Man, June, 1935, Vol. 1, No. 7, p. 3.

The editor asserts that the Negro should think independently, realizing that he must not only his manhood, but also his own racial or national prestige. It is only when he has successfully done this that the other people of the world will truly respect him and give him the honor due every man of courage and character.

49. "The American Negro." The Black Man, June, 1935, Vol. 1, No. 7, pp. 3 - 6.

The leader argues that the White man of America, like the White man anywhere else, is greatly influenced by wealth. The Negro must become wealthy. He must become a master of finance, a captain of industry, a director of science and art, an exponent of literature. He must develop a concrete philosophy, and with the combination of all these, he must impress himself not only upon American civilization, but upon the civilization of the world.

50. "The World As It Is." The Black Man, June, 1935, Vol. 1, No. 7, pp. 7 - 10.

The editor argues that the Negro must not depend upon the political promises of prospective members of Congress to enact an Anti-Lynching Law. The last ten years proved that there is no sincerity behind such a promise. Garvey states that politics has a great deal to do with the administration of the law and justice in the United States. One day America will pay for its sins---sins imposed upon the entire country by the cruel and criminal attitudes of the heartless and ignorant South. He declares that Negroes are depending on the League of Nations and world civilization to ignore any claims Hitler or Germany makes for the restoration of colonies in Africa. The leader asserts that Paul Robeson is a good actor but is being used by promotors to the dishonor and discredit of his race. Garvey declares that most of the cinema producers of every country are educating their public in prejudice against the Negro, so that the world-wide attitude is more immediately manifested with the cinema than through the old time agencies of propaganda.

51. "A Dialogue: What is the Difference?" The Black Man, June, 1935, Vol. 1, No. 7, pp. 10 - 12.

This is a dialogue between a son and father concerning racial prejudice against Black people. The son wanted to know why people speak and act disrespectably toward Blacks. The father pointed out that the Black Man has a great, glorious past but the history books left out their contributions; a Black Man is just an individual like anyone else, and individually, he can make himself what he wants to be. The father tells the son to be ever vigilant in the maintenance of the honor, dignity, and integrity of our race.

52. "Roosevelt and His Trouble." The Black Man, June, 1935, Vol. 1, No. 7, pp. 14 - 16.

Garvey points out that Roosevelt's trouble is with Congress. It wants to spend money and he wants to conserve spending. He declares that Roosevelt has made a gallant fight to serve his country and his people, but corrupt politicians handicap him and probably will defeat him.

53. "Garvey's First Message From London." The Black Man, June, 1935, Vol. 1, No. 7, p. 18.

He sees the Black man's cause as just and must he ever be vigilant in our own cause. The leader concludes that Black people are to reorganize their forces on the basis of better human understanding, and every unit of the race is asked to his/her duty. Each and everyone must realize that a serious obligation depends upon him.

54. "The Press and Its Influence." The Black Man, July, 1935, Vol. 1, No. 8, p. 1.

The editor asserts that Negro readers should not swallow blindly what is published in White newspapers. The Negro must learn to discriminate by properly analyzing what he reads.

55. "America and Abyssinia, Ethiopia ." The Black Man, July, 1935, Vol. 1, No. 8, pp. 1 - 2.

The leader urges American Negroes to use their political influence on President Roosevelt and on the members of the Senate and House to give any help that it can to Abyssinia against the aggression of Italy.

56. "The Future of The Negro." The Black Man, July, 1935, Vol. 1, No. 8, pp. 3 - 4.

The author argues that the purpose of the UNIA is to stir the Negro minds all over the world toward the glorious objective of the fulfillment of nature's design. He concludes that righteousness shall be our breastplate, the word of truth shall be our weapon, the Cross of Christ shall be our implement that those mighty races and nations shall not break through in the mighty rush of Negro hope and aspirations.

57. "A Barefaced Coloured Leader." The Black Man, July, 1935, Vol. 1, No. 8, pp. 5 - 8.

The writer is referring to W. E. B. DuBois. He called him the brazen fellow that one knows in Negro leadership. Garvey argues that DuBois assisted in having him imprisoned and deported. The leader said that when DuBois was active in the NAACP, it had no constructive program for Negroes and stood for nothing but complaints. Garvey concludes that the youth of American Negroes must dislodge men like DuBois from the assumptive positions of leadership and the effigy of him and his type should be placed alongside of that of Uncle Tom, because he has the same mentality.

58. "The World As It Is." The Black Man, July, 1935, Vol. 1, No. 8, pp. 9 - 11.

In this article Garvey discusses: "Britain's War Preparations," "Hitler and The Jews," "Roosevelt's Hands Tied," "War Industries Booming," "The War in Africa," "African and West Indian Negroes." Concerning the latter, the editor feels that the West Indian and African Negroes would do well to simulate the political astuteness of the American Negro, in that wheresoever they are, politics must form a very important role in their national lives.

59. "Sanity or Madness or Is It Blashemy?" The Black Man, July, 1935, Vol. 1, No. 8, pp. 11 - 13.

This article is about Father Divine. The writer states that he hopes that before any Negro joins Father Divine's new cult, he will count the cost physically, mentally, and spiritually, so that he may not entirely throw away his life. He concludes that to believe any man is God outside of the One True and Living God after one has been an adherent of real Christianity is so blasphemous as to suggest nothing else but a terrible penalty for such a person.

60. "The World As It Is." The Black Man, August - September, 1935, Vol. 1, No. 9, pp. 9 - 10.

The editor discusses: "Behavior of Whites and Blacks," "Jews in Congress," "A Negro Governor [For the Virgin Islands,]" "American Negroes at Geneva." Concerning the latter topics, Garvey asserts that both the British and French Negroes let their respective governments [England and France] know that they support Abyssinia in the Italo-Abssyninan question. He felt that the American Negroes were well represented in Geneva by Dr. Willis N. Higgins, a Black Man.

61. "Our Less - Remember It." The Black Man, August, September, 1935, Vol. 1, No. 9, pp. 11 - 12.

According to Garvey, Black people should have learned a lesson from World War I, and that Blacks should unite and use their political influence to bring about a change in the world. He argues that after wasting 20 years, the next 20 years must find Black people farther advanced toward the age when men of all races standing on equal platforms will point to their grand and noble deeds.

62. "The War." The Black Man, October, 1935, Vol. 1, No. 10, pp. 1 - 2.

The editor discusses the Italo-Abyssinian War and points out that the Abyssinians have not started to fight and they will be victorious in the end.

63. "Lest We Forget." The Black Man, October, 1935, Vol. 1, No. 10, pp. 3 - 4.

The leader argues that Black people all over the world are helpless to assist Abyssinia in her war against Italy. The main reason is that Black people are neither organized or united.

64. "The Negro and His Weakness." The Black Man, October, 1935, Vol. 1, No. 10, pp. 5 - 6.

Garvey contends that if Negroes are weak today---and we are weak---it is because of their past neglects, and the apparent gross negligence of the present. He concludes that Negroes should not succumb to their weaknesses, neither to that of the past or the present; we must recover and regroup ourselves and so the appeal is made to Negroes everywhere to make the determined effort to regain that noble consciousness that our ancient fathers once possessed.

65. "The World As It Is." The Black Man, October, 1935, Vol. 1, No. 10, pp. 8 - 11.

The editor discusses" "Barbarism in America," "A Haitian University," "Devastations in Jamaica," and "Paul Robeson Again." Regarding the latter, Garvey states that Robeson is not dignifying his race from the parts he plays in propaganda dramas. It is hoped that he is making enough money for himself so that when he retires from the stage he may be able to square his conscience with his race by doing something for it.

66. "The American Mind and The War." The Black Man, December, 1935, Vol. 1, No. 11, pp. 1 - 2.

Garvey declares that the politics of America is dominantly the ruling force in the life of the American people. He is referring to the Italo-Abyssinian War and America's support of the Italians.

67. "The Willingness To Do." The Black Man, December, 1935, Vol. 1, No. 11, pp. 3 - 4.

The writer contends that the Negro must make his own material life. Garvey concludes that Negroes must unite to bring into existence a new, improved civilization as to make it inviting to others because of its superiority.

68. "The Confusion in America." The Black Man, December, 1935, Vol. 1, No. 11, pp. 6 - 7.

The leader argues that among the Negroes of America, there are as many opinions and divisions of views as there are families among the 15,000,000. Every hundred Negroes have an organization of their own, and their leadership refuses to cooperate with or be a part of any other. He concludes that the greatest effort is to pull against each other - the surest way to weaken the strength of the race or the people. It is only by a proper understanding and a better reorganization will the American Negro rise to his position of higher usefullness, not only to himself, but to the rest of the race.

69. "Negro Waste." The Black Man, December, 1935, Vol. 1, No. 11, pp. 8 - 9.

The author points out that during the War, the Negroes made good money and bought homes, automobiles, diamonds, and pianos, but he paid inflated prices for them. Subsequently, the Negro lost everything he had.

70. "The War Begins." The Black Man, December, 1935, Vol. 1, No. 11, pp. 9 - 10.

The author is discussing the war between Italy and Abyssinia. He states that the Abyssinians will be victorious in the war.

71. "The World As It Is." The Black Man, December, 1935, Vol. 1, No. 11, pp. 11 - 12.

The editor discusses: "Hoare and Laval 'League Suicide,'" "A Colonial Law," "A West Indian Governor," "A Colonial Law," "Negro Politics in America," "Father Divine as God." Concerning the latter two topics, Garvey declares that the sensible Negroes have realized that it is only by playing the White man's politics in America, as he plays it, can they get anything out of it, and so they are playing it with vengeance and we compliment them. He states that those who are not in the immediate presence of Father Divine may treat the idea of his being God as a joke, but as a fact, there are people around him, in his presence, who really think that he is God, and some of them are not ignorant people.

72. "Germany Wants Colonies." "The Black Man, March, 1936, Vol. 1, No. 12, pp. 1 - 2.

The author argues that Black people all over the world are opposed to Hitler having colonies in Africa.

73. "Unpreparedness: A Crime." The Black Man, March, 1936, Vol. 1, No. 12, pp. 7 - 8.

The leader asserts that the Negro should disengage himself from the fantasy of exterior help and revert to his own initiative. He believes that Blacks should prepare with the vision of a people capable of seeing down through the ages. Garvey concludes that Blacks should prepare for the future.

74. "The World As It Is." The Black Man, March, 1936, Vol. 1, No. 12, pp. 13 - 14.

The editor discusses: "The French Colonies," "The British," "The Watch of the Rhine," "America and War," and Abyssinia and Peace." Regarding the latter topic, Garvey declared that Ethiopia should learn from the experience of the War with Italy that they cannot change their skin and that they are one with all the Negro people of the world.

75. "Communism and The Negro." The Black Man, May - June, 1936, Vol. II, No. I, pp. 2 - 3.

The writer feels that there is no difference between capitalistic White men and communistic White men in the determination of racial interest. He concludes that the Negro would be wasting time destroying one group for another, expecting much from the control of the new group, when as a fact all groups of Whites feel the same toward him.

76. "The Misfortunes of Haile Selassie." The Black Man, May - June, 1936, Vol. II, No. I, pp. 4 - 5.

This misfortune concerns Haile Selassie having to surrender the ancient scepter of Ethiopia. He was forced to do this because of the unpreparedness of Europe to meet the onslaught of the brutal spirit of Ethiopia-the spirit made manifest by the barbarian Mussolini.

77. "The World As It Is." The Black Man, May - June, 1936, Vol. II, No. I, pp. 5 - 7.

The editor discusses "The League of Nations," "British Home Government," "Italy's Abyssinian Bonds," "The West Africans," "The East Africans," "The West Indians," "South African Problems," and "The American Negroes." Regarding the latter, he declared that the next 50 years ought to mean much in the life of the American Negro, if his thoughts are directed in the proper channel. Garvey concludes that the Negro has much work to do. The Negro wastes no time in doing it. The rest of the Negro world is looking toward him with interest and anxiety.

78. "Educate! Educate! Educate!" The Black Man, May - June, 1936, Vol. II, No. I, pp. 7 - 8.

The leader believes that the leadership of the race all over the world today should concentrate on education as the primary factor in preparing the Negro for his new defensive position. He concludes that it is the duty of the Negro to develop a high state of intelligence superior to his adversary, and use that education for the means of extricating himself from the holes in which he is placed.

79. "A Warning to the Negro." The Black Man, May - June, 1936, Vol. II, No. I, p. 9.

The warning that Garvey gives is that the Negro must find a way to save himself. Without a positive program, without each and every man's sacrifice toward its realization, the race will be farther down, nearer its doom. He concludes that the Negro should get behind the program and if necessary, die for it.

80. "Italy's Conquest?" The Black Man, July - August, 1936, Vol. II, No. II, pp. 4 - 6.

The leader argues that Haile Selassie of Abyssinia allowed himself to be conquered by playing White, by trusting to White advisees, and by relying upon White governments, including the White League of Nations.

81. "The Peculiar Fear." The Black Man, July - August, 1936, Vol. II, No. II, p. 10.

This peculiar fear refers to Mussolini's training a colossal Black army in Africa. He concludes that if there should be any fear, the fear should be about the White man's army - the inhuman army of Italy, the unsparing army of Germany and the threatening army of Russia.

82. "The World As It Is." The Black Man, July - August, 1036, Vol. II, No. II, pp. 19 - 20.

The editor discusses: "Roosevelt's Challenge to America," "Schmelling and Joe Louis," "All Not Bad," "German Colonies in Africa," "The Patriots of Abyssinia," "The Negro in the USA." Concerning the latter topic, he argues that the knowledge that the Negro has gained must not only serve him in America, but must primarily serve him in rehabilitating the land of his fathers. The new world reorganization must include the Negro, all prejudice notwithstanding.

83. "Negroes Beware!" The Black Man, September - October, 1936, Vol. II, No. III, p. 2.

The writer is warning Negroes to beware of the Communists and Red Socialists who generally call themselves workers and are endeavoring to engage the Negro as a comrade in the fight against Capitalism.

84. "Look Up You Mighty Race." The Black Man, September - October, 1936, Vol. II, No. III, pp. 3 - 4.

The leader points out that Negroes had a glorious past and a grander day is before him. He lost his greatness because of the same miscarriage of things material and spiritual,as the White man now practicing in Europe. He concludes that with that double experience, we ought to be wiser in building anew. The Negro must look forward to things much better and much more beneficial than what we see today.

85. "Character! Character! Character: A Vital Necessity!" The Black Man, September - October, 1936, Vol. II, No. III, pp. 6 - 7.

The writer argues that the Negro needs character, real integrity, as his basic principle of life. He surmises that the Negro is in the process of building a civilization of his own. The foundation stone, therefore, must be basically character, intestinal fortitude, and integrity. Garvey concludes that without integrity, there is little hope, therefore, the Negro must practice integrity.

86. "The World As It Is." The Black Man, September - October, 1936, Vol. II, No. III, pp. 13 - 14.

The editor discusses: "Keep Italy Broke," "Abyssinia and The League," "West African Hope," East Africa in Doubt," "The United States as Teacher," and "The West Indies as Guide." Concerning the latter two topics, the editor argues that America is playing the role of teacher and the Negro students of the country must learn well and completely. When the day comes for a swinging of thought and action, the American Negro must be in the forefront to assume his racial responsibility. About the West Indies, Garvey believes that the Negroes in the islands have had more administrative experiences in business, industry, and government than any other group, not only in the Western Hemisphere, but of the world. He concludes that there is as much hope for the West Indies as for anywhere else in the outlook of the Negro toward nationalization and independence.

87. "Fighting in Abyssinia: The Emperor Runs." The Black Man, January, 1937, Vol. II, No. V, pp. 1 -

The editor states that the Negroes of the world have been very much interested in Abyssinia because it is a Black country even though the emperor did not think so. He concludes that the emperor's incompetence was shown primarily through his dependence upon people who were not his friends and who, therefore, could not advise him.

88. "The Negroes' Position." The Black Man, January, 1937, Vol. II, No. 5, p. 2.

The writer sees the greatest devil there is in the world today and the greatest hell that ever can ever suffered by man which constitute the conditions of poverty that deprives a man, race, or a people of honorable expression, actions, and comfortable existence. He concludes that such is the hell that the Negro suffers all over the world and the evil deity who presides over this condition is worshipped by those who refuse to rely upon their natural abilities to secure the things they desire.

89. "Paul Robeson and His Mission." The Black Man, January, 1937, Vol. II, No. V, pp. 2 - 3.

Garvey argues that Paul Robeson has appeared in motion pictures that do not reflect the dignity and credit due the Negro Race, and that he or any other Negro should only appear in motion picture that do reflect dignity and credit due the Negro Race.

90. "An English King and His People." The Black Man, January, 1937, Vol. II, No. V, p. 4.

The writer relates that the British government ridded itself of the most beloved king the English people had with his own consent, without the British people being cognizant of what was really happening. He is referring to ex-King Edward VIII.

91. "More Light on Haile Selassie." The Black Man, January, 1937, Vol. II, No. V, pp. 8 - 10.

The leader contends that Haile Selassie kept his country ill-prepared in a modern civilization whose policy was strictly aggressiveness. Garvey concludes that the Emperor resorted sentimentally to prayer, feasting, and fasting, which was not consistent with the policy that secured the existence of present-day freedom for people, while other nations and rulers are erecting armaments of the most destructive kind and the only means of securing peace and protection.

92. "Negroes Beware!!!" The Black Man, January, 1937, Vol. II, No. V, pp. 10 - 11.

Garvey warns Negroes to unite and beware of the exploitation of Whites and others. He concludes that Negroes must become responsible and appreciate the fact that until they begin to do for themselves no other sector of the world will be interested in doing for them that which is beneficial.

93. "The Negro and the Crisis." The Black Man, January, 1937, Vol. II, No. V, pp. 12 - 13.

The writer declares that the Negroes' reaction to Mussolini must be expectant of God to come down and draw the sword against the Italians but for the Negro himself to plan his own intelligent ingenuity by his reconquering his own country and in doing so, preventing others from doing unto him what Mussolini did to Abyssinia. He concludes that crises will appear again, as they have already come. Let the Negro be prepared for the changes in these crises.

94. "The World As It Is." The Black Man, January, 1937, Vol. II, No. V, pp. 15 - 16.

The leader writes about "The New Year," "Lady Houston," "Edward VIII and The Negro," "Germany and the Power Box," and "Roosevelt and The Americans." Regarding the latter topic, the editor argues that Roosevelt made a trip to South America to cement the friendship and fellowship of the American Republics. He concludes that this is a wise move and can well be understood under the leadership of a man as studious and philosophical as Franklin D. Roosevelt.

95. "Haile Selassie and Benito." The Black Man, March - April, 1937, Vol, II, No. VI, pp. 1 - 2.

The editor surmises that Blacks cannot compliment Haile Selassie for having had more than 10 ,000,000 slaves in Abyssinia, neither can we compliment Benito Mussolini for conquering the country with the sole purpose of exploiting the Abyssinians in the interest of the Italians. He concludes that Selassie is no better than Mussolini.

96. "The Negro Problem in South Africa." The Black Man, March - April, 1937, Vol. II, No. VI, p. 3.

It is pointed out that South Africa compares in racial prejudice to the Southern part of the United States. He concludes that as much as some White South Africans would like to erect a barrier against the advancement of the Negro, nature has her own way of demolishing these barriers.

97. "The African At Home And the African Abroad." The Black Man, March - April, 1937, Vol. II, No. VI, pp. 6 - 7.

The writer declares that the African at home and abroad should now soberly settle upon a policy that will allow him to regain and reestablish his mighty power. He concludes that the Negro must aspire to his inspirations and integrity by spearheading all that comprises the glory and honor of human civilization.

98. "The Failure of Haile Selassie As Emperor." The Black Man, March - April, 1937, Vol. II, No. VI, pp. 8 - 9.

The writer believes that when the historical data regarding Haile Selassie of Abyssinia is compiled, it will depict him as a coward who exiled himself from his country thus saving his own skin, and leaving millions of his countrymen to struggle through a deplorable war that he helped to create. This was a result of his political ignorance and racial disloyalty. Garvey concludes that Selassie has not proven his nobility in the war between Italy and Abyssinia.

99. "Plain Talking To The Negro." The Black Man, March - April, 1937, Vol. II, No. VI, pp. 9 - 10.

Garvey declares that the Negro must venture out and in so doing, become independent: become his own erector, architect, captain, and his own leader. He concludes that the Negro must see things only from his point of view, while at the same time, respecting the points of view of other men. Garvey's point of view must be the only supreme, ultimate objective.

100. "The World As It Is." The Black Man, March - April, 1937, Vol. II, No. VI, pp. 17 - 18.

The editor discusses: "The French Make Negro Governor," "A Question From Nigeria," "Get Out Of Our Weakness," "The American Negro In Sports," and "Negro Judges In America." Regarding the latter two topics, the writer surmises that in the realm of boxing, the Negro has elated the status of Blacks. He argues that presently (1937), there are two Negro municipal judges - Charles E. Toney and James S. Watson, in Harlem, who have been reflecting the highest credit due the Black Race.

101. "Fooling The Negro." The Black Man, August, 1937, Vol. II, No. VII, pp. 5 - 6.

The writer argues that too many people exploit Negroes. Black Men in Africa, the West Indies, and South and Central America, and the United States should concert themselves in rank and concentrate upon the dignity and integrity of the race. He concludes that the past glories can be duplicated in the present and guarantee the future, if Blacks would only summon their ancient pride and courage that once made them the masters of the universe.

102. "A Racial Weakness." The Black Man, August, 1937, Vol. II, No. VII, pp. 7 - 8.

The leader contends that we must save all that we earn, all that we possess - and we must religiously and scrupulously determine what values we can bequeath our children and guarantee their generations.

103. "The World As It Is." The Black Man, August, 1937, Vol. II, No. VII, pp. 15 - 16.

The editor discusses the following topics: "Solomon's Mines," "Abyssinia," "South Africa," "Scottsboro," and "Dice and the Negro." Concerning the latter two topics, Garvey states that the State of Alabama reduced the sentence of four of the six Scottsboro Boys who were imprisoned for rape for six years. The boys were falsely accused of the crime. Regarding the latter, the writer avers that the English Press was indulgently casting ridicule and deranged contempt so permanently desired so as to establish his socio-economic and political inferiority. He concludes that these things should be desisted.

104. "Building A State." The Black Man, March, 1938, Vol. III, No. IX, pp. 3 - 4.

The leader argues that the building of a state is the first duty of the race. He contends that the Black man's only hope and redemption for the future is the erection of that state for which he can wield the power that nature intends for every group.

105. "The Negro and His Future." The Black Man, March, 1937, Vol. III, No. IX, pp. 6 - 7.

The writer surmises that the Negroes' future is dependent upon themselves. They can view it through no other eyes than their own. Garvey concludes that only the present deeds of the Negro will depict the future.

106. The Unsteady World." The Black Man, July, 1938, Vol. III, No. X, pp. 3 - 4.

Garvey surmises that the Negro must exert more of his intellectual and penetrative energies. His rewards must be consistent and diplomatic. He concludes that this is the type of leadership that is needed in order to redeem the Negro in this unsteady world where things are pendulous - a reach that is bound to strike the unknowing opponents a decisive blow in the head. The Negro must exert sober leadership that will pilot him throughout the most contemptuous era of his existence.

107. "Riots in Jaimaica and British Guiana." The Black Man, July, 1938, Vol. III, No. , pp. 5 - 7.

The author points out that the riots were the result of the unrest of the laborers refusal to work because of the poor working conditions and salaries. He concludes that the laborers will not revert to their past conditions before the strike.

108. "The World As It Is." The Black Man, November, 1938, Vol. III, No. II, pp. 18 - 20.

The author discusses: "Senator Bilbo's Bill," "Royal West Indian Commission." "The Jews in Palestine," "The West Indian," and "The American Negro." Regarding the latter two topics, Garvey declares that it is fervently hoped that the West Indians will continue taking their stances as a race and, in so doing, fight for their future. With this outlook, the two elements of the Negro Race in the West may unite forces with the Africans. In time they may be able to establish themselves not as a subjective race, but as one of the dominant races in the universe. Garvey concludes that the American Negro is the natural leader of all Negroes of the world and his leadership must be negated if the utmost diligence is not undertaken in the conquest of the ultimate, universal progress of the race.

109. "The Negro and the African." The Black Man, February, 1939, Vol. IV, No. I, p. 4.

The editor discusses the significance of the word "Negro" and "African." He states that it is disheartening in that a healthy, prepossessing race such as the African or Negro Race should not appreciate the meaning by which people are described. This various names identify and depict the Black Race as being individually different from other groups. He concludes that the term "Negro," is a healthy, strong term and Negro leaders should be proud of it, strengthen it, and dignify it.

110. "The World As It Is." The Black Man, February, 1939, Vol. IV, No. I, pp. 19 - 20.

The editor discusses: "Portugese Africa," "Sir Stafford Cripps," "Labour in Jamaica, BWI," "Joe Louis and the Germans," and "White and Black." Regarding the latter two topics, the author surmises that Joe Louis was designated as the wild "monster" by the Germans because he gave Max Schmelling, a German, a good thrashing. Concerning "White and Black," Garvey argues that let the Negro and other oppressed people realize that it is by force and strength and their ability to retaliate does a race become recognized. Let the Negro learn to adamantly defend himself.

111. "The World As It Is." The Black Man, June, 1939, Vol. IV, No. I, pp. 10 - 11.

The editor discusses the "West Indian Cricket Team," "South Africa," "Roosevelt and The World," "The Pope," and "Jamaican Riots." Concerning the latter three topics, Garvey states that, unfortunately, no President of the United States can speak of justice of the world without having the Negro question thrown into his face. Although Roosevelt is recognized as a very capable leader, and one who did his best for the American Negro, it must be realized that he is still President of a nation whose hands are unclean. Concerning the Pope, Garvey surmises that the Pope blessed the Italian Facist invaders of Abyssinia, which the Pope interpreted as "an act not consistent with the Vicar of Christ on Earth." Concerning the "Jamaican Riots," the editor feels that the riots were the result of the Jamaican workers wanting better wages and working conditions.

3
MAJOR BOOKS

---

112. Burkett, Randall K. *Black Redemption: Churchmen Speak for the Garvey Movement*, Philadepha: Temple University Press, 1978.

All of the churchmen spoke in behalf of the Universal Negro Improvement Association although they did share a mutual set of attitudes regarding the Black church, the racial situation in the United States, and the relationship of Black America to Africa. The speeches and sermons by the churchmen stand as testimonials to Garvey's ability to appeal to a wide spectrum of Black church leaders into support of a program that surpassed the bounds of strict demonination. There is a short biographical sketch of each of the ten churchmen as well as their speeches and sermons. One of the churchmen includes a woman - Emily Christmas Kinch - who was a missionary in Africa.

113. ______. *Garveyism As A Religious Movement: The Institutionalization of A Black Civil Religion*, Metuchen, NJ: Scarecrow Press and The American Theological Library Association, 1978.

The author discusses "Religious Ethos of The UNIA," "Garvey As Black Theologian," "Sect or Civil Religion: The Debate with George Alexander McGuire," and "Clergy in The UNIA." The clergy in the UNIA include Baptists, AME, AME Zionists, CME, Episcopalians, Black Jews, Methodist Episcopalians, and the Congregational Church. The writer argues that Garvey took seriously the religious character of the movement he spearheaded and he articulated a remarkably well-developed, internally consistent theological framework by which to interpret the meaning of his peoples' history and their destiny under God who was working in their behalf.

114. Clarke, John Henrik, Editor. Marcus Garvey and the Vision of Africa, with the assistance of Amy Jacques Garvey, NY: Vintage Books, 1974.

A collection of articles and documents by and about Marcus Garvey. The editor of this reader shows that Garvey's popularity was universal. His program, the return of African people to their motherland, shook the foundations of three empires; all subsequent Black Power Movements have owed a debt to his example and his prophecy has been fulfilled in the independence that brought into being more than 30 African nations. This book has Extensive Notes, Bibliography, and Index.

115. Cronon, Edmund David. Black Moses: The Story of Marcus Garvey and The Universal Negro Improvement Association, Madison: University of Wisconsin Press, 1969.

This is the standard work on Marcus Garvey. The author surmises that Garvey's protest took the form of a complete rejection of the White world through an escapist program of chauvinistic Black nationalism. Cronon believes that Garvey is significant because in the early 1920s, at least, Garvey symbolized the longings and aspirations of the Black masses. The writer concludes that Garveyism failed largely because it was unable to produce a viable alternative to the unsatisfactory conditions of American life as it affected Blacks. Escape, either emotional or physical, was neither a realistic nor lasting answer. Extensive References, Notes, and Index are included in this work.

116. ______, Editor. Great Lives Observed: Marcus Garvey, Englewood Cliffs, NJ: Prentice-Hall, Inc., 1973.

This is a collection of writings on and by Marcus Garvey. Part One, "Garvey Looks At the World." Part Two, "The World Looks At Garvey." Part Three, "Garvey in History." There is also a Chronology of the Life of Marcus Garvey, Bibliographical Note and Index.

117. Davis, Daniels. Marcus Garvey, NY: Franklin Watts, Inc., 1972.

The writer points out that the symbols of Black Pride: "natural" hair, African clothes, the red, green, and black buttons, phrases like "Black is Beautiful," --- all have their roots in the mass movement led by Marcus Garvey and his message of racial nationalism. The writer declares that Garveyism, whether one accepts its particulars or not, points the way for the future of Black Movements in its emphasis on building mass support of the poorest and most deprived people in the Black community. Before Garvey, Black-led Movements depended upon the educated elite or the middle class for their followers. The new mood of the 1970s makes it clear that a successful Black thrust for equality must draw its support from the masses of poor Blacks and must concern itself with the issues THEY define as important to their lives. The writer concludes that Garvey's faults, like his failures, were many. He made his mark upon his times and his influence remains strong in his own day, and will, in all probability, grow stronger. There are a number of photographs of Garvey, his wife, Amy Jacques Garvey, Ku Klux Klan, UNIA, and Black leaders such as Robert Abbott, A. Philip Randolph, Kwame Nkruman, and Malcolm X along with a Selected Bibliography and Index are included in this text.

118 . Edwards, Adolph. Marcus Garvey: 1887 - 1940, London: New Beacon Books, 1967.

This terse 43 page book attempts to give a factual exposition of Garvey rather than an analytical critique. The writer surmises that it is more meaningful to state the facts and allow the reader to make his own evaluation as to Garvey's work and as to his place in history. The book is divided into the following main headings: "Early Life," "Work in the United States," "Work in Jamaica," and "The Garvey Legend." The author concludes that there are two lessons that can be learned from Garvey: the immense value of a mass movement and the tremendous importance of the press as a publicity organ. There are more than 115 Footnotes included in this work.

119 . Fax, Elton C. Garvey: The Story of A Pioneer Black Nationalist, NY: Dodd, Mead, and Company, 1972.

The author attempts to see Garvey as part of the fabric of the environment. His environment stage teems with human souls no less revealing than he. Some are noble; others are far less noble. The writer declared that Garvey still stands as one of modern history's great personalities and dynamic visionaries. The charges he leveled in his day at the United States are equally valid today. Whenever and wherever the dark slums and their irate tenants bubble amid festering, hopeless squalor, the ghost of Marcus Garvey haunts the premises. Fax concludes that in the haunting, one hears the echoing exhortations answered by the cry mingled with the terrible snarl and that is the collective voice of those convinced that the ONLY thing they have to lose is the misery of their obscurities.

120. Garvey, Amy Jacques, Editor. <u>Philosophy and Opinions of Marcus Garvey</u>, NY: Arno Press and The New York Times, 1969. Originally published in 1923 and 1925.

This work includes Marcus Garvey's major speeches on his indictment and conviction by the United States Government. He also lashes out at those he considered his enemies such as W. E. B. DuBois, the NAACP, the Communists, Black Intelligentsia, and the Intelligentsia, and the interference of well-meaning liberal Whites. The major emphasis in his speeches was that Black people must unite and organize themselves.

121. ______. <u>Black Power in America: Marcus Garvey's Impact on Jamaica and Africa</u>, Kingston, Jamaica: The Author, 1968.

The writer argues that Marcus Garvey was the forerunner of the "Black Power" and "Black Is Beautiful" Concepts in the United States. She asserts that there is a connection between her husband's teaching and the philosophy of Elijah Muhammad and Malcolm X. Mrs. Garvey also declares that Garveyism was one of the main ingredients that helped to set the African independence Explosion into motion.

122. Maglangbayan, Shawna. <u>Garvey, Lumumba, and Malcolm: National-Separatists</u>, Chicago: Third World Press, 1972.

The author contends that Garvey marked the opening of the Twentieth Century with one of the greatest revolutionary movements that the Black World has known. He pointed the way to the Black Man's liberation. Yet, we did not acclaim him enough, as if his life has been peripheral to our very existence. The writer points out that it took two decades after his death for Lumumba and Malcolm to follow his footsteps and, once again, point us in the direction we should go. This book attempts to give the world a corrective view of what each man stood for , why they did what they did, and in which direction they were headed.

123. Manoedi, M. Korete. <u>Garvey and Africa</u>, NY: New York Age Press, 1922.

The author, a South African and son of a Chief in Basutoland, was critical of Garvey and his Movement. The author attempted to warn of suspicion of the Garvey Movement. He contends that the Garvey Movement was simplistic and ill-conceived. Manoedi points out that not all Africans favor Garvey's Movement of transporting Black Americans to Africa.

124. Martin, Tony. Race First: The Ideological and Organizational Struggle of Marcus Garvey and The Universal Negro Improvement Association, Westpoint, CT: Greenwood Press, 1976.

The author contends that no one could have organized and erected the largest Black Movement in Black History, in the face of continuous onslaughts from Communists on the left, Black Reactionaries on all sides, and the most powerful governments in the world, and yet be a buffoon or clown, or even an overwhelmingly impractical visionary. This study attempts to treat Marcus Garvey and The Universal Negro Improvement Association with the seriousness and respect due them. An Appendix of UNIA Branches in the United States, Photos, Illustrations, Extensive Bibliography, and Index are included.

125. Mudgal, Hucheshwar G. Marcus Garvey: Is He the True Redeemor of the Negro? NY: H. G. Mudgal, 1932.

The author believes that Marcus Garvey was an honest man and that he expressly, capably, and passionately remonstrated the monstrous ills and wrongs to which the African populations are subjected, the entire scale of socio-economic oppression, the enslavement of Africans on reserves where the land is of the worst quality, the infamous code of South African Pass Laws, the equally infamous wage contracts, the disfranchisement of Black voters, etc. The writer concludes that---for better or worse---Garvey has aroused the Negroes' thinking in terms of self-respect, integrity, dignity, freedom, equanamity, and racial pride.

126. Nembhard, Lenford. Trials and Triumphs of Marcus Garvey, Kingston: Gleaner, 1940.

This was the first full length Biography of Marcus Garvey. The writer was praiseworthy of Garvey and focused on his activities in Jamaica following his deportation from the United States.

127. Vincent, Theodore G. Black Power and the Garvey Movement, Ramparts Press, NY: 1971.

The writer contends that Garvey's first concern was the building of a nation and anyone who stood in the way of this struggle was to be opposed, whatever economic theory he espoused. According to the author, Garvey would be classified as a "welfare-state liberal." Furthermore, Garvey was far more concerned with the evils of imperialism than with domestic economic policies. Vincent declares that like Black Power Advocates of today, Garvey could conceive of only two versions of the future---either the Black Man could receive his freedom---or war would be inevitable.

Vincent, Theodore G.

The writer concludes that Garvey's objective was to give to Blacks a consciousness of the nationhood which already existed and to conduct this effort without being jailed, assassinated, or exiled.

4
GENERAL BOOKS

---

128. Alvarez, Joseph A. From Reconstruction to Revolution: The Blacks' Struggle for Equality, NY: Antheneum, 1971.

The author contends that Marcus Garvey did not intend for all American Blacks to return to Africa. Garvey points out that some Blacks were no good here in America and naturally will be no good in Africa. He wanted American Blacks to help build a strong, independent Africa that would give prestige and strength to Blacks everywhere.

129. Barrett, Samuel. The Need of Unity and Cooperation Among Colored Americans, Oakland, CA: Voice Publishing Company, 1946.

The author declares that Marcus Garvey was beyond question, the greatest organizer and the most inspirational leader the Black Race ever produced. Barrett continues to write that Black History does not record a single instance of any man comparable to him in this respect. The fidelity of his followers, and the extent and scope of his operations placed him on a pedestal that no other Black has ever attained, surmises the writer. The author gives three reasons why the Garvey Movement failed. First, Garvey made a great mistake in not having as his associates a cabinet of worthy and outstanding Black Americans and together map out a plan of procedure and actions instead of attempting to do it alone or delegating certain powers to men who were not qualified. Second, the Garvey Movement failed "through intrigue on the part of the Firestone Interests, and W. E. King, who paid certain intellectual Blacks in the United States

Barrett, Samuel.

to spread propaganda inimical to the Movement." Third, it failed "on account of the envy, jealousy, and internective welfare on the part of some of the officials and leaders within the organization." Those officials and leaders lacked unity of aim and concerted efforts coupled with racial pride concludes Barrett.

130. Bennett, Lerone, Jr. Pioneers in Protest, Chicago: Johnson Publishing Co., Inc., 1968.

Marcus Garvey is included in this collection of protest leaders. The writer asserts that Garvey was an agitator/organizer, perhaps the best one produced in Black America. He concludes that although Garvey's Movement was a failure insofar as neither he nor any of his followers ever settled in Africa. Nevertheless, Garvey left behind him living monuments and is considered the Prophet of Black Nationalists of America and the Leader of the emerging states of Africa.

131. Bontemps, Arna and Conroy, Jack. Any Place But Here, NY: Hill and Wang, 1966.

The authors contend that the palpable failure of Garvey's grandiose schemes had a deflating effect on the enthusiasm of followers who had been charmed by his silver tongue. In addition, he made some questionable references which could be interpreted as, at least, a left-handed endorsement of the Klu Klux Klan's argument that the United States should be made "a White man's country." The writers argue that although Garvey had a grandiose and bombastic scheme, it was sincere and had some practical features.

132. Boulware, Marcus H. The Oratory of Negro Leaders: 1900 - 1968, Westport, CT: Negro Universities Press, 1969.

Chapter Five is entitled, "The Marcus Garvey Period: 1916 - 1927." The writer contends that Garvey's ability to capture the attention of listeners on "short exposure" projected him as a man of ability and diligence. When Garvey advocated something, his voice had a sincere ring, and the audience were given the impression that he himself was sold upon it. When he was anti-anything, the listeners thought it must be bad. The author concluded that like Jesus Christ, Garvey had the voice of authority and "the people heard him gladly." Garvey's mannerisms and personality begat loyalty and commanded respect.

133. Brimberg, Stanlee. Black Stars, NY: Dodd, Mead and Co., 1974.

There is one section in this collection on Marcus Garvey. The writer points out that Garvey never got to see his dream come true. He had awakened hundreds of thousands of Black people. No longer would they camouflage themselves with light-colored makeup under White hair styles. No longer would they be ashamed of their color. Garvey had shown them that "Black is Beautiful" and they had their own history and that it was a beautiful history. The writer concluded that for the first time in America, they walked tall, like Marcus Garvey had, Black and Proud.

134. Brisbane, Robert H. The Black Vanguard: Origins Of The Negro Social Revolution, 1900 - 1960, Valley Forge, PA: Judson Press, 1970.

Chapter Four in this work discusses, "The Era of Marcus Garvey." The author gives a Biographical Overview of his life from his birth in 1887 to his death in 1940. He surmises that Garvey's first public appearance in the United States was in the role of a soapbox orator on the streets of Harlem in the company of some of Harlem's first Negro demagogues and chauvinists. By 1919, Garvey was already the most talked about Negro in the world. Brisbane points out that some Garveyites were to be found among the early recruits of the Black Muslims of the 1930s. He concludes that the meteoric flash of Garvey's rise awed even his most bitter enemies, and some of the more thoughtful among them, eventually paid him the respected tribute of emulation.

135. Brotz, Howard. Negro Social and Political Thought: 1850 - 1920, Representative Texts, Edited by Howard Brotz, NY: Basic Books, 1966.

There is one section in this work entitled, "The Revival of Political Nationalism: Marcus Garvey." Several articles were taken from The Negro World, a weekly newspaper in which Garvey often expressed his views. The articles include: "Race Assimilation," "The True Solution to the Negro Problem," "An Appeal to the Soul of White America," "Racial Reforms and Reformers," "Who and What Is A Negro?", "An Appeal to the Conscience of The Black Race to See Itself," "The Negroes' Place in World Reorganization," "Aims and Objects of Movement for Solution of Negro Problem," and "Racial Ideals."

136. Coombs, Norman. The Black Experience in America, NY: Twayne Publishers, Inc., 1972.

The writer surmises that although Garvey had, overnight,

Coombs, Norman.

created the largest Mass Organization in Afro-American History, it crumbled almost as quickly as it had been built. Furthermore, declared Coombs, the Movement had been overly dependent upon his personality. However, Garvey cannot be dismissed so easily. The author concludes that although his Movement disintegrated rapidly, the interest in Black identity and Black pride which he had sparked, lingered on. Lacking a structure within which to operate, it was not very obvious to the external observer. Nevertheless, his ideas have clearly provided the spawning ground from which more recent organizations have developed.

137. Cox, Earnest Sevier. Lincoln's Negro Policy, Los Angeles, CA: The Noontide Press, 1968.

There is one section entitled "Marcus Garvey." The author points out that the Garvey Movement succeeded in doing what other Black Repatriation Movements had failed to do---it gained the attention. Garvey's imprisonment deprived him of active leadership. His exile from the United States separated him from the largest group of his followers, and the world-wide depression also served to reduce the organization's great membership. It continues, however, and is rebuilding a large membership.

138. Cox, Oliver C. Race Relations: Elements and Social Dynamics, Detroit: Wayne State University Press, 1976.

There is one section in this work entitled "Marcus Garvey as Nationalist." The writer argues that the most persuasive Black Nationalist and Racist, Marcus Garvey, came to the fore during World War I, the period of the great universal efflorescence of nationalism when racism, in general, was first brought into serious contention. Mr. Cox argues that Garvey encouraged Whites to be racist so that his own Black racism might be justified and accepted by American Blacks. He concludes that there were three immediate reasons for Marcus Garvey's decline: (1) He was dealing with an essentially fictious world. The Black nations - Liberia, Haiti, Ethiopia - were not impressed by his programs; (2) He apparently misunderstood the nature of the culture with which he was dealing. The British Imperial System that he proposed to duplicate among African Blacks was not accepted by Marcus Garvey states but by private enterprise; and (3) His exaltation of Blackenss, regarded as his residual contribution had to be skin deep. In reality, "Black Is Beautiful," only insofar as Black Behaves Beautifully." Blacks or Whites can behave beautifully only to the extent that they are culturally prepared to do so.

139. Cruse, Harold. Rebellion or Revolution? NY: William Morrow & Co., Inc., 1968.

The author contends that the DuBois - Garvey dispute was over economic issues and not ideologies. He points out that the DuBois - Garvey conflict was more concerned with leadership tactics than with certain racial principles involved in such goals as "Back to Africa," "civil rights," and "nationalism." The writer also argues that the Garvey Movement was a Revolutionary Nationalism being expressed in the very heart of Western Capitalism. Despite the obvious parallels to Colonial Revolutions, however, Marxists of all parties not only reject Garvey, but have traditionally ostracized Negro Nationalism.

140. Davie, Maurice R. Negroes in American Society, NY: McGraw-Hill Book Co., 1949.

The author suggests that the Garvey Movement was based upon good psychology. It made the downtrodden lower class Negroes feel like somebody among White people who said they were nobody. It gave the crowd an opportunity to show off in colors, parades, and self-glorification. The author concludes that as a Negro Chauvinistic Movement with political implications, the UNIA was doomed to failure, for it could not gain White support. As a movement in the development of race consciousness and racial pride, however, it had enduring significance. Garvey demonstrated that it is possible to reach the Negro masses if they were appealed to in an effective way.

141. Davis, Daniel S. Struggle for Freedom: The History of Black Americans, NY: Harcourt Brace Jovanovich, Inc., 1972.

The writer contends that Garvey's short-lived Movement of Black people in history and his charismatic leadership rallied millions to his cause, but once he was removed from the scene, it melted away. His hard core supporters continued to preach Black Nationalism, and Garvey's influence continues to this day as such groups as CORE openly describe themselves, as Garvey, who offered emotional release from the burdens of being Black in a nation that still preached White supremacy; but he did not offer a reasonably realistic program that would lead to Black progress, nor did his constant attacks on Black leaders and lighter-skinned Blacks help to bring about the unity Blacks so desperately needed.

142. Davis, King E. Fund Raising in the Black Community: History, Feasibility, and Conflict, Metuchen, NJ: Scarecrow Press, 1975.

Davis, King E.

The author contends that in 1916, the most famous Black fund raising movement developed---Marcus Garvey's Black Nationalist Movement - The Society for Universal Negro Improvement. The author concludes that although the Garvey Movement did not succeed, it had an influence on the Black Muslim Movement, which now uses some of the methods and techniques Garvey developed for raising funds from low-income populations.

143. Dennis, R. Ethel. The Black People of America: Illustrated History, NY: McGraw-Hill, 1970.

The author declared that Garvey's message gave hope to people who had found only unemployment, segregation, and violence in the "promised land" of the North. The writer surmises that The Universal Negro Improvement Association (UNIA) collapsed because it lacked sound financial management. More basically, states Dennis, the Movement disappeared because its goals of transporting millions of Black Americans to Africa was impractical. As a symbol, however, Garvey continued to be popular with Blacks long after his death in 1940.

144. Deusen, John George. The Black Man In America, Washington, DC: Associated Publishers, 1944, Revised Edition.

The author surmises that although opposed by many of the greatest Black leaders, Garvey raised more money in a few years than any Black organization ever dreamed of. Garvey understood the psychology of Black people. He knew that an exploited and underprivileged group desired to forget its condition of poverty in dreams of pomp and splendor.

145. Dowd, Jerome. The Negro in American Life, NY: The Century Co., 1926.

The writer argues that Whites consider the Garvey Movement as a mere chase after the rainbow, but he considered it important matter in every respect that is creditable to its leader, and to all who are backing it. He concludes that Garvey's dream will never be realized, but his efforts may result in providing a refuge for his people when they begin to feel the struggle for existence here too unequal and too cruel.

146. Draper, Theodore. The Rediscovery of Black Nationalism, NY: Viking Press, 1969.

The author asserts that Garveyism came closest to expressing itself in terms of traditional nationalism. It made "nationhood" the highest ideal of all peoples. The trouble was that Garvey's proposed Negro nation was in Africa, whereas his constituency was in the

Draper, Theodore.

United States. Draper concludes that Garveyism was an authentic American Negro Movement in the guise of an African fantasy. Garvey appealed mainly to recently uprooted Negro migrants from the Southern states and recently arrived immigrants from the West Indies, who were stirred emotionally by an exotic incarnation of nationalism and emigration, even a spurious nationalism and an imaginary emigrationism.

147. DuBois, W. E. B. Dusk of Dawn: An Autobiography of A Race Concept, NY: Harcourt, Brace, and Co., 1940.

The author was an archenemy of Garvey and declares that Garvey's Movement was a grandiose and bombastic scheme, utterly impractical as a whole, but it was sincere and had some practical features; and Garvey not only proved to be an astonishing popular leader but also a master of propaganda. Within a few years, news of his movement, of his promises, and his plans reached Europe and Asia and penetrated every corner of Africa.

148. ______. The Autobiography of W. E. B. DuBois, NY: International Publishers, 1968.

The writer recalls that he had heard of Marcus Garvey while he was in Jamaica in 1915. Garvey sent DuBois a letter welcoming him to Jamaica in behalf of the United Improvement and Conservation Association.

149. Essien-Udom, E. U. Black Nationalism: A Search For An Identity in America, Chicago, IL: University of Chicago Press, 1962.

The wrtier contends that Garvey's ideology was both nationalist and racist. His nationalist objective was the redemption of Africa for "Africans abroad and at home." He advocated racial purity, racial integrity, and racial harmony. The major instrument for achieving Garvey's objectives was economic cooperation through racial solidarity. Garvey was also interested in politics. The Negro Political Union was established in 1924 to "consolidate the political union of the Negro through which the race would express its political opinion." This was Garvey's latter day adventure into domestic politics of the United States. During the presidential election of 1924, Garvey issued a list of approved candidates and came out strongly in support of Calvin Coolidge, the Republican presidential nominee.

150. Educational Book Publishers, Inc. Afro-American Encyclopedia, North Miami, FL: Educational Book Publishers, Inc., 1974, Vol. 4.

Educational Book Publishers, Inc.

The authors contend that Marcus Garvey gave Blacks new founded hope and new purpose. He was the new Negro of the 1920s, which was a period of rebirth in the cultural life of Black people.

151. Foner, Eric, Editor. America's Black Past: A Reader in Afro-American History, NY: Harper & Row, 1970.

Africa for Marcus Garvey symbolized the past and future greatness of the Black race and his emphasis upon the African homeland was part of his greatest stress on pride in Blackness. Garvey's interest in Africa was one of expression of a rising tide of Pan-Africanism in the 1920s. The author concludes that nationalist movements like Garvey's succeed because they give Blacks a sense of meaning in their lives and an identification with a power center which is proudly non-White and openly challenges White domination.

152. Foner, Philip S. American Socialism and Black Americans: From the Age of Jackson to World War II, Westport, CT: Greenwood Press, 1977.

One selection in this work is entitled "Garvey Must Go!" The author discusses the "Marcus Garvey Must Go" campaign of the Socialist Party, as being spearheaded by A. Philip Randolph and Chandler Owen, inasmuch as the Black Socialist editors, Randolph and Owens were among Garvey's earliest associates in Harlem. The editors argued that not only was Garvey's ideology false, but it seriously hindered the march of Black radicalism. They also felt that Blacks were finally beginning to be radicalized, to demand justice, and to be accepted by organized labor, and along came Marcus Garvey to divert them from all this and from their fundamental problems in American society, with his "pipe dreams" of Africa. Randolph and Owen concluded that Garveyism only widened the gap between Black and White workers, the only result of which would be more racial hatred and ultimately more racial violence.

153. Foster, William Z. The Negro People in American History, NY: International Publishers, 1970.

Chapter 41 discusses "The Garvey Movement." The author contends that the Universal Negro Improvement Association (UNIA) was a Negro bourgeios nationalist movement, a sort of Negro Zionism; and Garvey was a bourgeois nationalist leader. Garvey's was the voice of the Negro petty bourgeoisie, seeking to secure the leadership of the Negro people by subordinating their national feelings and needs to class interests. The author discusses Garvey from a Marxism-Leninism view point.

154. Franklin, John Hope. From Slavery to Freedom: A History of Negro Americans, NY: Random House, 1975.

The writer suggests that the effects of Marcus Garvey's doctrines on the unlettered and inexperienced Negro urban element, recently removed from the farm, was magnetic. He was hailed by thousands as the true leader of the Negro Race. Dr. Franklin argues that the widespread interest in Garvey's program was more of a protest against the anti-Negro reaction of the post-war period than an approbation of the grandiose schemes of the Negro leader. He concludes that the significance of the Garvey Movement lies in the fact that it was the first and only real mass movement among Negroes in the history of the United States and that it indicates the extent to which Blacks entertained doubts concerning the hope for first-class citizenship in the only fatherland of which they knew.

155. Frazier, E. Franklin. The Negro in the United States, NY: McMillian & Co., 1949.

The writer argues that as a leader of a mass movement among Negroes, Garvey has had no equal. On the whole, Garvey was able to utilize the frustrations and disillusionments of the urbanized Negro masses to weld them into a mass movement. The appeal of the Garvey Movement was really opposed to the other worldly outlook of the Negro church. However, Garvey was shrewd enough to not challenge Negro ministers and to utilize the religious heritage of the Negro. He concludes that the emergence of the Garvey Movement was an extreme expression of race consciousness and nationalistic sentiment which came into prominence during and following World War I.

156. ______. Black Bourgeoisie, Glencoe, IL: Free Press, 1957.

The author argues that although the Garvey Movement had its largest following in New York City, it spread to Chicago, Detroit, and Philadelphia, and even attracted some Negroes in Southern cities. Dr. Frazier suggests that the Garvey Movement did not attract any support from the emerging Black bourgeoisie. He concludes that the Black bourgeoisie not only regarded his programs as fantastic, but they did not want to associate with his illiterate and poor Black followers, especially since West Indians were prominent in the Movement.

157. Fulks, Bryan. Black Struggle: A History of the Negro in America, NY: Dell Publishing Co., 1969.

The writer argues that it was in the dark ghetto setting of squalor, frustration, and despair that the

Fulks, Bryan.

Garvey Movement flashed so brilliantly during the Twenties. Fulks further declares that Marcus Garvey, a man with a wonderful creative imagination and a remarkable ability to attract people and money, came to New York from his native Jamaica. He concludes that in the course of a few years he collected far and wide an estimated $10 million, established cooperatives, and factories, built the Black Star Steamship Lines, and organized a private army.

158. Gilbert, Peter, Editor. The Selected Writings of John Edward Bruce: Militant Black Journalist, NY: Arno Press and The New York Times, 1971.

There is a letter in this work to Marcus Garvey from John Edward Bruce. In this letter dated August 17, 1920, Bruce refused nomination as President of the American Sector of the UNIA, but assured Garvey that he was in complete accord with all of the aims and aspirations of the organization. Another section in this book is entitled "Marcus Garvey and the UNIA." This is an article Bruce wrote defending the integrity of Marcus Garvey. One other article also dealt with Garvey. In 1918, when Garvey returned to the United States after touring Europe, Bruce recorded his first impressions of the man. His impressions were unfavorable. Later his opinions changed and he became one of his most trusted lieutenants.

159. Glenn, Norval D. and Bonjean, Charles M. Blacks in the United States, San Francisco, CA: Chandler Publishing Co., 1969.

The authors point out that although Garvey's goals were somewhat unrealistic and the Movement ultimately failed, Garvey was important because "he left legacy of attitudes and beliefs which continue to motivate, or at least influence the behavior of a Black Protest Segment which is as yet outside the mainstream of Black protest." Garvey taught his followers to distrust the White man and to rely solely upon their own efforts to better their conditions. Furthermore, he exalted his followers to take pride in being Black and to develop solidarity as a race.

160. Gosnell, Harold F. Negro Politicians: The Rise of Negro Politics in Chicago, Chicago, IL: University of Chicago Press, 1935.

The author points out that the Garvey Movement from time-to-time took an active part in politics. In Chicago, this Movement, with its "Back to Africa" slogans and its appeals to racial pride, was able to turn over a considerable number of votes to certain

Gosnell, Harold F.

Negro candidates. In the 1924 Primary in the First Congressional District, the Movement was active for the Negro candidate.

161. Grant, Robert B. The Black Man Comes to the City: A Documentary Account From the Great Migration to the Great Depression, 1915 - 1930, Chicago, IL: Nelson-Hall Co., 1972.

The author contends that it was not Marcus Garvey's concern for Africa alone that makes his role an important one. Garvey's contribution lay in his ability to stir the Black masses to develop racial pride where only frustration had existed and to convey to tens of thousands of followers a sense of the power that was theirs if they could work together, concluded the writer.

162. Hall, Raymond L. Black Separatism in the United States, Hanover, NH: University Press of New England, 1978.

Chapter Four discusses Marcus Garvey and "Militant Black Nationalism." The author argues that Marcus Garvey was the UNIA's sole architect and the Movement's values, in essence, reflected only slight differences from those of mainstream America. Garvey advocated many of the same principles that America did: racial pride, justice, and world order, economic security, and self-determination. The author concludes that Garvey's Movement centered on his charisma and its impact can best be gauged by the spin-off effects it produced. That Garvey had millions of followers proves that he offered what the Black masses wanted, and this fact was not lost on those who controlled power; for White Americans, the myth that Blacks could not organize and have visions of freedom in America, as well as elsewhere, could never be the same. For many Black Americans in search of a way out of the oppressive restraints of White power, Garvey and Garveyism served as a model for Ideological and Utopian Black Liberation.

163. Harris, Janet and Hobson, Julius W. Black Pride: A People's Struggle, NY: McGraw-Hill Book Co., 1976.

The author surmises that although Marcus Garvey's visions were impractical, and his dreams were escapist, after Garvey, Black people never felt quite the same about themselves. Marcus Garvey made Black people proud of their Race. In a world where Black is despised he taught them that "Black is Beautiful."

164. Haywood, Harry. Negro Liberation, NY: International Publishers, 1948.

The author suggests that the mass movement led by Garvey cannot be explained solely by the personality of its leader. Garveyism represented a convergence of two social forces. On the one hand, it was the trend of the recent migrants from the peasant South. On the other hand, Garveyism reflected the ideology of of the Negro petty bourgeoisie, their abortive attempt at hegemony in the Negro Movement. The author concludes that the Garvey Movement was destined to failure. Some the factors which caused this were: the subsiding of the economic depression; the ushering in of the "boom" period, with the subsequent easing of the plight of the Negro people; the growing adjustment of Negro migrants to their new environment, and their increased integration into industry.

165. ______. Black Bolshevik: Autobiography of an Afro-American Communist, Chicago: Liberator Press, 1978.

The writer contends that although the Garvey Movement attracted the lower class of the Black community, it also attracted small businessmen, shopkeepers, property holders, professionals, doctors, lawyers, etc. A major role in the Movement was also played by deeply disillusioned Black veterans who fought an illusory battle to "make the world safe for democracy" only to return to continued and even harsher enslavement. The author asserts that the main contradiction inherent in the Garvey Movement from its inception had been the conflict between the needs of the masses to defend and advance their rights in the USA and the fantastic Back to Africa schemes of the Garvey leadership. He concludes that Garvey's emphasis upon these schemes reflected his resolution of the conflict in favor of business interests and against the interests of the masses.

166. Henri, Florette. Black Migration: Movement North, 1900 - 1920, Garden City, NY: Doubleday and Co., 1975.

The writer believes that Garvey appeared at precisely the time they were most ready to embrace any program that would give substance to their new sense of pride, self-respect, and racial consciousness, and that promised an escape from riots, lynchings, and the mundane. Garvey committed a serious error contends the author. In 1922, he astounded the Black community by meeting with the Imperial Giant of the Klu Klux Klan in Atlanta. Garvey's reasoning was the fighting the Klan would only create racial strife and turmoil because most White Americans shared Klan prejudices. Since the Klan wanted to rid themselves of Blacks, why not enlist the Klans' support in removing Blacks to Africa?

Henri, Florette.

The writer concluded that migration, urbanization, education, a wage-earning, and finally, the war with its broadening of horizons and heightening of expectations, made the Garvey Movement possible.

167. Huggins, Nathan I., et al., Editors. Key Issues in the Afro-American Experience, NY: Harcourt, Brace, Jovanovich, Inc., 1971.

There is one chapter, "The Flowering of Black Nationalism: Henry McNeal Turner and Marcus Garvey," by Edwin S. Redkey that discusses Garvey. The writer argues that both Turner and Garvey tried to learn about Africa; and their visions of an independent, powerful African nation were more than empty dreams. The author concludes that the flowering of Black Nationalism under Bishop Turner and Marcus Garvey sowed seeds that are still growing. First, the promise of African freedom inspired Africans to work for independence from Europe Second, the stress of Black accomplishments erected a new pride in the Afro-American lower class that would one day blossom into a new Black power and independence.

168. Jenkins, Robert E. The Negro in American Life and History: A Resource Book for Teachers, San Francisco, CA: Unified School District, 1967.

There is a section entitled, "Marcus Garvey and Black Nationalism." The writer argues that between 1914 - 1932, Marcus Garvey became a symbol and spokesman for more than one million Blacks. Garvey founded the UNIA in 1916, which had over six million followers. DuBois and the NAACP saw Garvey as a threat to their movement and Whites ignored the Garvey Movement altogether. Blacks considered the movement to be opportunistic and demagogic in the use of uniforms, parades, and rituals to obtain members. The Communist Party adopted a "self-determination" policy for Blacks which claimed to be consistent with Lenin's philosophy on racial and cultural minorities.

169. Kardiner, Abram and Ovesey, Lionel. The Mark of Oppression: Explorations in the Personality of the American Negro, NY: World Publishing, 1972.

The authors surmised that as crude as were Marcus Garvey's methods and and as unsound his rational background, he saw one important truth: that the Black man was doomed as long as he took his ideals from the White man. He saw that this cemented his internal feelings of inferiority and his self-contempt. The writers concluded that Garvey was wrong only in the means he used to liberate the Black man from it.

170. Kornweibel, Theodore, Jr. No Crystal Stairs: Black Life and the Messenger, 1917 - 1928, Westport, CT: Greenwood Press, 1975.

Chapter Five discusses "The Garvey Must Go Campaign." The writer contends that the Messenger was a leading voice on the anti-Garvey Campaign, and while not the sole publication that took upon itself to expose the West Indian organizer, it kept up what was probably the most continuous attack. Once the Messenger seized on the Garvey issue, it did not relent until the public was only a few steps away from the federal penitentiary in Atlanta, Georgia, argues the author.

171. Kusmer, Kenneth L. A. Ghetto Takes Shape: Black Cleveland, 1870 - 1930, Urbana: University of Illinois Press, 1976.

The author believes that Garveyism was more important as a cultural phenomenon than as a social movement. The Garvey Movement was essentially the lower-class counterpart of the bourgeois "New Black" phenomenon. Garvey's rhetoric struck a responsive chord in the Black masses of the 1920s because it perfectly reflected the essential ambivalence that resulted from enhanced economic opportunity accompanied by the growth of the ghetto and increased discrimination. The writer declared that in many ways Garvey's economic and political ideas differed little from the mainstream conversation of White America in the 1920s. Until the race could erect its own enterprises, Garvey preached, Black workers should shun unions and look to their employers as their best friends. The author concluded that perhaps Garvey best summarized the ambivalent identity of his followers when he selected a name for this proposed independent Black Nation in Africa. "The United States of Africa," he called it.

172. Lincoln, C. Eric. The Black Muslims in America, Boston: Beacon Press, 1961.

Marcus Garvey's Movement was essentially political and social. He did not base his doctrines and program upon any religious premise. Yet, he did not neglect the wellspring of religious fervor---and discontent---in the Black community. The author concludes that Garvey's own stature continues to grow as more and more observers concede that, for all his faults, he had a profound awakening effect on the Black American community. Furthermore, continues Dr. Lincoln, Garveyism lives on not really as a Movement, but as a symbol---a symbol of the militant Black Nationalism which so many Black Americans see as their only alternative to eternal frustration and despair.

173. Logan, Rayford W. and Cohen, Irving S. The American Negro: Old World Background and New World Experience, Boston: Houghton-Mifflin Co., 1970.

The authors concluded that the Garvey Movement was doomed to failure. The majority of Blacks had no desire to "return" to Africa because they had never been there. America was their native land and they did not intend to leave it. European nations, however, would never allow Garvey's followers to settle in their African colonies and spread discontent among their subjects. Finally, Garvey lacked the skill and finesse mandatory in carrying out his program. The authors declared that Garvey's personal failure was not as important as the damage he did to Blacks' quest for freedom. He left an undeniable legacy of racism---of anti-White hatred---that has influenced a growing portion of the Black community. Worst of all, concluded the writers, he stirred bitter feelings between dark and light-colored Blacks, between American-born and West Indian Blacks. This disunity played right into the hands of those who regarded all Blacks as their enemies.

174. Lubell, Samuel. White and Black: Test of a Nation, NY: Harper and Row, 1964.

The author contends that the Garvey Movement must be looked upon as much more that escapist theatricals. He argues that many of the themes of Garveyism as a rejection of White society persist in Negro thinking and feelings. Lubell concludes the glorification of the color Black, the emotional identification with African independence, efforts to organize Negro owned and operated businesses, drives to "buy Black" retreats into self-segregation---all of these agitations were first expressed by Garvey. He also stated that although Garvey, A CATHOLIC, never repudiated Christianity fully; he did criticize it as the religion that White men "preach and will not practice."

175. Lyons, Thomas T. Black Leadership in American History, Reading, MA: Addison-Wesley Publishing Co., 1971.

Chapter Four is entitled, "Marcus Garvey: Leader of Black Nationalism." The author surmises that racial pride was the basic ideology of Garvey. Back to Africa was the other basic element in Garveyism. The writer points out that Garvey urged the Whites to give Africa self-determination, and he repeatedly said that he held no hostility and that he contemplated no violence against Whites. There is a Bibliography at the end of the chapter.

176. McKay, Claude. Harlem: Negro Metropolis, NY: E. P. Dutton & Co., Inc., 1940.

Chapter Ten is devoted to "Marcus Aurelius Garvey." He contends that Garvey himself had no intention of going back to live in some corner of the vast land of his ancestors. He extorted Negroes to trade among themselves, to make contacts for trading with Negroes abroad, to start a real Negro Church based upon African religion, erect Negro schools, and a society of Negro people. Garvey wanted to create a Negro society according to the European plan, with royalty, nobility, laity, priests, and workers. The writer argues that the flowering of Harlem's creative life came in the Garvey Era. If Marcus Garvey did not orginate the phrase, "New Negro," he at least made it popular. McKay concludes that Garvey should not be compared to Hitler or Al Capone. He was not a common criminal, or kidnapper, and murderer of babies.

177. Meier, August and Rudwick, Elliott. From Plantation to Ghetto, NY: Hill and Wang, 1970.

The writers contend that Garvey dramatized, as no one before had done, the bitterness and alienation of the Black masses. Thus, the Garvey Movement provided a compensatory escape for Blacks to whom the urban promised land had turned out to be a hopeless ghetto. It is significant, however, that the relationship between Black migration and nationalist ideologies was not a new one. The authors conclude that the Garvey Ideology and Movement were part of a larger pattern associated with migration tendencies among Southern Blacks.

178. Mezu, S. Okechukwu and Desai, Ram. Black Leaders of the Centuries, Buffalo, NY: Black Academy Press, Inc., 1970.

There is one chapter in this collection on "Marcus Garvey and African Nationalism." The authors surmised that nearly every work on African Nationalism has asserted the influence of Garveyism on the growth of race consciousness in Africa. While Garveyism did not have any permanent influence, the available evidence suggests that it ignited more interest and controversy and was a more powerful utopia among African Nationalist groups than the DuBois' (Pan-African) Movement. Garvey's ideas not only reached nationalist circles in West Africa and South Africa, they also reached French-speaking Africans and West Indians in Paris in the 1920s. The writers also conclude that although Garvey's Movement had no direct contact with Equatorial Africa, French and Belgian officials were prone to attribute any local disturbances in their colonies to Garveyism and to the Pan-American Movements in general.

179. Morris, Milton D. The Politics of Black America, NY: Harper and Row Publishers, 1975.

The author surmises that Garvey's advocacy of mass migration to Africa by Blacks was less a desire to escape Black subordination here than a desire to erect a Black empire that would provide strength, dignity, and pride for Black people everywhere. The writer concludes that the grand migration which Garvey promised never occurred, but he came closer than anyone else to providing a measure of fulfillment to the dream.

180. Morsbach, Mabel. The Negro in American Life, NY: Harcourt, Brace, and World, 1967,

The writer believed that the popularity of the Garvey Movement was based upon the fact that it encouraged Blacks to express a pride in their race. The author surmises that few of the followers of Garvey had any real intention of moving to Africa. Blacks had a long tenuous history of helping to build America, and most had no wish to leave their native land. Furthermore, concluded the writer, they hoped to stay here did not rid themselves of racial discrimination in their own country.

181. Moses, Wilson Jeremiah. The Golden Age of Black Nationalism: 1850 - 1925, NY: Archon Books, 1978.

The writer states that the reactionary elements in Garveyism cannot be denied. Garvey's attitude toward miscegenation was worse than an accommodation to racism; it was an invitation to participate in racism, and it was a direct endorsement of laws that were written to dehumanize Black people. He argues that Garvey's Pan-Africanism was a modification of an existing movement, rather than a new creation. The author concludes that Garvey hewed out a strong, rough-edged and honest expression of Black Nationalist consciousness in which the formerly isolated Elitist Black Nationalism was mingled with the exuberance of the less articulate masses of newly urbanized Negroes.

182. Mulzac, Hugh. A Star To Steer By, NY: International Publishers, 1963.

The author was Captain of Marcus Garvey's ship, the Black Star. This book discusses how he became involved in the Garvey Movement. He points out that Garvey was a great organizer, but a poor business man. Mulzac discusses how and why the Black Star failed. It was due to poor business management.

183. Myrdal, Gunnar. An American Democracy, NY: Harper and Row, 1962.

The author argues that the Garvey Movement proves that it IS possible to reach the Negro masses if they are appealed to in an effective manner. It testifies to the basic unrest in the Negro community. It suggests that the effective method of lining up the American Negroes into a mass movement is a strongly emotional race-chauvinistic protest appeal. He concludes that the Garvey Movement illustrates---as the slave insurrections did a century earlier---that a Negro Movement in America is doomed to ultimate dissolution and collapse if it cannot gain White support. This is a real dilemma. For White support will be denied to emotional Negro chauvinism when it takes organizational and political forms.

184. Nielson, David Gordon. Black Ethos: Northern Urban Negro Life and Thought, 1890 - 1930, Westport, CT: Greenwood Press, 1977.

The author called Marcus Garvey a racial Zionist who came to the United States in 1916 and who accepted at face value the ever present White expressions of prejudice---as did the ordinary Black American. The writer concludes that at the same time racism continued to demonstrate to many the correctness of Garvey's assertion that Black Americans had no future in their own country. White Americans ironically "discovered" the Negro---or rather, the "New Negro."

185. Nkrumah, Kwame. Autobiography of Kwame Nkrumah, NY: Thomas Nelson & Sons, 1957.

The writer points out that Marcus Garvey had a tremendous influence on his life. He concludes that of all the literature he had studied, the book that did more than any other to fire his enthusiasm was the Philosophy and Opinions of Marcus Garvey.

186. Ottley, Roi. Black Odessey: The Story of the Negro In America, London: John Murray, 1949.

The author surmises that by his amazing energy and daring, Garvey excited the imagination of Negroes. He raised more money in a few years than any other Negro organizer ever dreamed possible. Ottley argues that although Garvey's doctrine, rituals, and Negro history and officialdom gave a sorely driven people a new sense of dignity, Negroes had no intention of leaving the United States. He concludes that Garvey might not have been convicted of mail fraud except for his determination to conduct his own case and his tendency to strut before a crowded courtroom.

187. Ottley, Roi. New World A-Coming, Boston, MA: Houghton-Mifflin, 1943.

The writer declared that the Garvey Movement set in motion what was to become the most compelling force in Black life, race and color consciousness, which is today (1943), what ephemeral thing that inspires 'race loyalty:' the banner to which Blacks rally, the chain that binds them together. The author surmises that the movement propelled many a political and social movement and stimulated racial internationalism. Ottley concludes that the Garvey Movement was indeed a philosophy, an ethical standard by which most things are measured and interpreted. The writer also saw Garvey's Movement as accounting for much of the constructive belligerency today (1943).

188. ______ and Weatherby, William J, Editors. The Negro in New York, NY: Oceana Publications, Inc., 1967.

The authors argue that Garvey left behind him a residue of profound racial consciousness which he had aroused in Negroes. They point out that in 1937, Garvey declared Mussolini and Hitler had stolen his idea, as "we were the first Fascists, when he had one hundred thousand disciplined men and women and were training children." The writers concluded that Garvey is more than anyone else responsible for the beginning of anti-Semitism among the Negroes.

189. Padmore, George. Pan-Africanism or Communism? Garden City, NY: Doubleday and Company, 1972.

The author declares that Garvey's vanity was his own undoing. He made enemies where he should have cultivated friends. Furthermore, surmises Padmore, had he been less boastful and more tactful, he might well have gotten a foothold in the Negro Republic, and not only have helped to stimulate economic development, but also have established a base for his nationalistic activities throughout Africa. The writer concludes that despite his obvious limitations as a diplomatist and statesman, Garvey was undoubtedly one of the greatest Negroes since Emancipation, a visionary who inspired his race in its upward struggle from the degradation of centuries of slavery.

190. Peeks, Edward. The Long Struggle for Black Power, NY: Charles Scribner Sons, 1971.

The author contends that had Garvey been able to maintain his United States base, the Movement no doubt would have been forced to shed fantasies about empire-building. In time, it would have taken on more of the realities of the Black American community for better health and housing and for job development and

Peeks, Edward.

commercial enterprise. The writer surmises that Garvey demonstrated, although not always wisely, what the Black masses could do to right the social, political, and economic injustices imposed upon them. He appealed to their pride, strength, and determination to oppose such wrongs with positive deeds and group enterprises.

191. Pinkney, Alphonso. Black Americans, Englewood Cliffs, NJ: Prentice-Hall, 1975.

Marcus Garvey organized the Universal Negro Improvement Association, a multifaceted organization with millions of members and 900 chapters throughout the world. The activities of the UNIA were much more than economic: its ideology combined territoriality-cultural, and religious nationalism-with economic nationalism. The writer concludes that UNIA became the first organization to embrace the complete spectrum of Black nationalism, and its leader was the first Black man to develop a comprehensive ideology of Black Nationalism.

192. ______. Red, Black, and Green: Black Nationalism in the United States, NY: Cambridge University Press, 1976.

Chapter Three is devoted to "Marcus Garvey and the Universal Negro Improvement Association." The author argues that the creation of racial pride among Blacks throughout the world no doubt is the most profound and lasting contribution of Garvey and the UNIA. The major thrust of Garvey's cultural nationalism took the form of teaching pride in Blackness, racial solidarity, and respect for the African declared heritage of Black people. The writer declared that Garvey did more than anyone else to stimulate the racial pride and confidence among the Black masses. He concludes that this important legacy has been passed on to the present generation of Afro-Americans and their counterparts in numerous African countries, including the Central African Republic, The Congo (Zaire), Ghana, Kenya, Nigeria, and Zambia, all of which have achieved political independence since his death and whose leaders have acknowledged his inspiration.

193. Ploski, Harry A., et al., Editors. Reference Library of Black America, NY: Bellwether Publishing Co., Inc., 1971.

Editors contend that Marcus Garvey, like Malcolm X of a later generation, believed that Blacks could never achieve equality unless they became independent---founding their own nations and governments, their own businesses and industrial enterprises, their own military establishments---in short, those same institutions

Ploski, Harry A., et al., Editors.

by which other peoples of the world had risen to power.

194. ______. and Brown, Roscoe C., Jr. The Negro Almanac, NY: Bellwether Publishing Co., 1967.

The authors point out that critics of Garvey are quick to label him a pretentious crank, whereas his supporters are equally disposed to call him an unqualified genius. From a more historically impartial viewpoint, surmise the writers, he must be regarded as a kind of fanatical visionary---a utopian who undertook enormous and grandiose schemes---a man literally driven by the notion that Blacks' sole means for achieving a unique culture in the Twentieth Century was through the foundation of a unified separatist empire in Africa. The authors concluded that although his ideas, in their ultimate form, may have been rejected by most of his day, it is clear that since then, these very same ideas---in a different perspective---have had a favorable influence on the policies of many Black leaders the world over.

195. Powell, Adam Clayton, Jr. Marching Blacks, NY: Dial Press, 1945.

The author argues that Marcus Garvey was one of the greatest mass leaders of all time. He concludes that Garvey was misunderstood and maligned, but he brought to the Black Race, for the first time, a sense of pride in being Black.

196. Quarles, Benjamin. The Negro in The Making of America, NY: Collier Books, 1964.

The author suggests that Marcus Garvey was a self-dramatizer as well as a man of amazing energy and persuasion. He established himself in Harlem, New York in the 1920s and literally catapulted himself into the limelight. Dr. Quarles argues that with a sure sense of mass psychology, Garvey utlized plumed hats and cockades, street parades, with brass bands, playing martial airs, "African Redemption," medals, and the conferring of such titles of nobility as "Knight" and "Duke." He concludes that the imagination of Negroes was excited by something more than his showmanship. He appealed to their vanity and craving for power.

197. Record, Wilson. The Negro and the Communist Party, NY: Antheneum, 1971.

The writer points out that at first the Communists were not opposed to the Garvey organization. They were anxious to develop a race and national consciousness among Blacks as well as to ally the race with the working class. The Party was greatly impressed by

Record, Wilson.

the lower-class appeal of the UNIA. Though Communists were keenly disappointed in the shift in emphasis toward "Negro Zionism," they were sorry to see the Movement die. The Garvey Movement was failing. The Communists maintained, because it had succumbed to the pressures of the bourgeoisie; it had deviated from the basic policy laid down at its 1920 convention and was now placing its whole emphasis on a "Back to Africa" program. The UNIA, according to the Party, could be salvaged only by a concentration of its energies around the fight for equality for Blacks within the United States. While Party members within the UNIA were under orders to force acceptance of this latter program, they were so few in number as to be ineffective. Record concluded that the fact that Blacks had responded to the Garvey Program helped to change the Communists minds in the United States and in the Kremlin.

198. Redding, Saunders. <u>They Came in Chains</u>, Philadelphia, PA: J. B. Lippencott Co., 1950.

The writer argues that the Garvey Movement cannot be dismissed merely as the aberration of an organized pressure group. The least that can be said of it is that it was an authentic folk movement. He concludes that its spirit of race chauvinism had the symphathy of the overwhelming majority of the Negro people, including those who opposed its objectives. This was the potent spirit of race consciousness and racial pride that informed the "New Negro."

199. ______. <u>The Lonesome Road: A Narrative History of Blacks in America</u>, Garden City, NJ: Doubleday, 1958.

The writer points out that ten million dollars was collected by the Garvey Movement from 1919 to 1921. The author concludes that Garvey went to Europe where in 1940, he died---too wretched to remember how profoundedly he had stirred the racial consciousness of Colored people throughout the world, and too senile to realize how firmly he had anchored the pride and passion of America's "New Negro" in the hurrying wave of the future.

200. Reid, Ira De. A. <u>The Negro Immigrant: His Background , Characteristics, and Social Adjustment, 1899 - 1937</u>, NY: Columbus University Press, 1939.

The author declares that the Garvey Back to Africa Movement was based upon elements of racial individuality and embodied sentiments which spring out of the life experiences of Negroes. As a mass movement, it satisfied the vanity and longing for something to give

Reid, Ira De. A.

meaning to the lives of thousands of Negroes. He concludes that the movement was essentially one of escape. It survived because it gave those newly urbanized group status in a White world where they were nobodies.

201. Rogers, Joel A. World's Great Men of Color, Vol. II, NY: MacMillan Publishing Co., Inc., 1972.

Marcus Garvey is discussed as one of the "World's Men of Color." Rogers argues that Garvey had all the potentialities of a Hitler or a Mussolini. His cause was just but his methods were distorted, archaic, and perverse contends the writer. He undoubtedly wanted to help the downtrodden Blacks but like every other autocrat, believed that the end justified the means. The author points out that Garvey had very little or nothing of the millions of dollars he had taken in. Rogers concludes that Garvey aroused millions of Blacks and Whites in many lands to think of the "Race" problem as they had never before. Because of this, he will be remembered and idealized more and more as time passes by.

202. Roome, William J. W. Aggrey: The African Teacher, London: Marshall, Morgan, and Scott, n. d.

The author argues that J. E. Kwegyir Aggrey, an influential leader, denounced Garvey and his Movement. Aggrey discouraged Africans from supporting Garvey.

203. Sitkoff, Harvard. A New Deal for Blacks: The Emergence of Civil Rights As A National Issue, NY: Oxford University Press, 1978.

The author contends that decrying the futility of the Negro struggle for emancipation in the United States, Garvey mocked the NAACP's campaigns against lynchings and disfranchisement. He urged Afro-Americans to abstain from politics and to invest their funds into the UNIA's Black Star Steamship Line and other all-Negro business enterprises. The author concludes that Garvey was an intuitive psychologist and a persuasive teacher that convinced masses of Negroes that White racism and not Black failures explained their lowly status. Years after his deportation in 1927, some of Garvey's most bitter Black enemies would be utilizing this legacy to forge a powerful campaign for civil rights.

204. Slik, Jack R. Van Der. Black Conflict With White America: A Reader in Social and Political Analyses, Columbia, OH: Charles E. Merrill Publishing Co., 1970.

Slik, Jack R. Van Der.

The author contends that when Garvey established the Universal Negro Improvement Association and Africans Communities League in New York City in 1917, he brought Integral Nationalism to a people who were searching for hope in what appeared to be a hopeless situation. Mr. Slik asserts that Garvey's integral form of Black Nationalism flourised in a situation where White Northerners feared that Blacks would deprive them of their jobs. Its significance was not only that it was the first major social movement among the Black masses, but it also indicated the extent to which they "entertained doubts regarding the hope for first-class citizenship in the only fatherland of which they knew." He concludes that the Garvey Movement DID NOT show the dualism found in earlier nationalist sentiment. It was a philosophy that fully embraced Blackness and vigorously rejected White America.

205. Spear, Allan H. Black Chicago: The Making of A Negro Ghetto, 1890 - 1920, Chicago, IL: University of Chicago Press, 1967.

The writer points out that Garvey made his first debut in Chicago in 1919. Garvey used this visit to bolster membership in the newly formed Chicago branch of the UNIA and to promote his latest scheme---an all-Negro steamship company that would link the Black peoples of the world. The Garvey Movement faced serious difficulties in Chicago. He surmised that Garvey's flamboyant nationalism had won him bitter enemies. Because of this, Robert Abbott waged a vigorous campaign against him. The author concludes that Garveyism flourished in Chicago for several years.

206. Thuku, Harry. An Autobiography, Nairobi: Oxford University Press, 1970.

The Kenyan nationalist recalls how he was influenced by Garvey. The writer also sought Garvey's advice and help. Thuku was jailed by the British for his nationalist drive for independence for Kenya. Garvey sent a letter to the Prime Minister of Britain protesting Thuku's imprisonment.

207. Twombly, Robert C. Blacks in White America Since 1865: Issues and Interpretations, NY: David McKay Co., 1971.

The author surmises that a combination of circumstances brought about Garvey's decline: strong opposition from Black Americans like DuBois who thought him a charlatan; his own inept business practices, especially with the Black Star Line; and harassment from the federal government resulting in his conviction for mail fraud in

Twombly, Robert C.

1923 and his indictment for income tax evasion in 1924 all culminated in his deportation as an undesirable alien in 1927. The author concluded that charlatan or not, he elevated the level of racial consciousness of the Black masses, created a nationwide organization that undoubtedly strengthened racial pride, and left a irtal undeniable legacy that, at the very least, contributed to the separatist philosophy of Malcolm X. Garvey also helped to make White America more color conscious than at any other time since Reconstruction.

208. VanDeusen, John G. The Black Man in White America, Washington, DC: Associated Publishers, 1944.

The writer contends that Garvey understood the psychology of the Negro. He knew that an exploited and underprivileged group desires to forget its conditions of poverty in dreams of pomp and splendor. This is what Garvey gave the people. The author states that Garvey admonished Negro peoples everywhere to overthrow White sovereignty. He concludes that there were probably not half a dozen educated Negroes in America who were genuinely interested in Garvey's proposition.

209. Warner, Robert A. New Haven Negroes: A Social History, New Haven: Yale University Press, 1940.

The writer mentions that the Garvey Movement attracted followers in New Haven. A branch of the Universal Negro Improvement Association and a store were opened in New Haven. A few Negroes abandoned their church affiliations and joined Garvey's African Orthodox Church. The author concludes that while the West Indians, Garvey's compatriots, were particularly attracted, the mass of Black New Haveneans were uninterested, amused, or hostile.

210. Weisbord, Robert G. Genocide? Birth Control and the Black American, Westport, CT: Greenwood Press, 1975.

The author surmises that Garvey seems to have said little about birth control per se but he was concerned about the tragedy of racial extinction. He wanted his Universal Negro Improvement Association (UNIA) to strengthen the Black Race so as to eliminate the possibility that Blacks would be exterminated. Garvey planted the seeds of the "Black is Beautiful" philosophy which was espoused and germinated in the Black Revolution of the 1960s. Garvey, of course, did not live to see that happen.

211. Weiss, Nancy J. The National Urban League: 1910 - 1940, NY: Oxford University Press, 1974.

The writer suggests that the Urban League recognized Garvey only in the pages of Opportunity and there he received sparse attention. The Garvey portrayed and depicted in the pages of Opportunity was a posturer and a charlatan, at once a "dynamic, blundering, temerarious visionary," and the master manipulator of the Black masses. Garveyism, as Opportunity depicted it "was a dream world escape for the 'illiterate' from the everlasting curse on their racial status in this country." The author concludes that while the Urban League disdained Garvey's methods, it recognized the value of its goals of racial harmony, consciousness, identity, and a sense of racial pride.

212. Wells, Ida Barnett. Crusade for Justice: The Autobiography of Ida B. Wells, Alfreda M. Duster, Editor, Chicago: University of Chicago Press, 1970.

The author knew Marcus Garvey personally. She points out that if Garvey had the support which, in her words, his wonderful Movement deserved, and had he not become inebriated with power too soon, there is no predicting what the result would have been. Mrs. Wells also delivered an address at one of the meetings of the Universal Negro Improvement Association in which 3,000 people were in attendance. She concludes that she told Garvey that his shipping company would only be successful if he had competent people.

213. Wesley, Charles H. The Quest for Equality: From Civil War to Civil Rights, NY: Publishers Co., Inc., 1968.

There is one section on "The Garvey Movement." The author surmises that Garvey instilled into Blacks a sense of racial pride of their ancestry by stressing the military, political, and artistic triumps of their heritage. He emphasized the Beauty of Blackness telling of a Black God and Black Christ, a Black Virgin Mary, and Black Disciples. Garvey also focused his attention on the international scene. He sent a delegation to the Versailles Peace Conference, asking that the German colonies be granted to his African government. They, of course, rejected his request.

214. Young, Henry J. Major Black Religious Leaders: 1755 - 1940, Nashville, TN: Abingdon Press, 1977.

Marcus Garvey is discussed here as a religious leader. The author argues that Garvey did not think of God as a reality detached and removed from the Black Liberation Struggle. He conceived God as a reality whose metaphysical nature made his existence an integral

Young, Henry J.

part of the liberation struggle. Garvey developed theological organically in light of such sustaining ideas as self-assertions, independence, self-determination, nationhood, courage, strength, love, justice, righteousness, and corporate consciousness. The writer concludes that all of Garvey's theological motifs were geared toward the actualization of the liberation of unified Blacks throughout the universe.

5
MAJOR ARTICLES

---

215. "A Garvey Myth." <u>Messenger</u>, Vol. 5, November, 1923, pp. 861 - 862.

This article shattered the myth that Marcus Garvey had organized more Blacks than any other Black leader. It noted that he had gotten more money and done less with it than any other Black leader. This article cites the many Black businessmen which were dependable, trustworthy, and really beneficial to their race.

216. "A Negro Moses and His Plans for An African Exodus." <u>Literary Digest</u>, Vol. 68, March 19, 1921, pp. 48 - 51.

This article discusses Garvey's plans for a Black nation in Africa and centers around statements made by Garvey to a writer for <u>The Independent</u>, a New York newspaper. The bulk of this article is composed of statements from the interview. Garvey discusses such things as the fact of his Blackness and Black Pride, his reasons for waiting to mobilize Blacks, Africa, and the work of the Black Star Line and the UNIA.

217. "A Symposium on Garvey." <u>Messenger</u>, Vol. 4, December, 1922, pp. 550 - 552.

Chandler Owens, Executive Secretary of the Friends of Negro Freedom, sent a questionnaire to 25 prominent Blacks to obtain their thoughts on Marcus Garvey. It noted that Garvey had met with Klu Klux Klan leaders and A. Philips Randolph's receipt of a human hand accompanied by a letter from the Klan telling him to join the Garvey Organization. Questions asked were: if the respondent thought Garvey's Policy was correct for Blacks and if they thought he should be deported.

The respondents included: W. E. B. DuBois, Carl Murphy, Carter G. Woodson, Archibald Grimke, Emmett J. Scott, and Kelly Miller.

218. Akpan, M. B. "Liberia and the Universal Negro Improvement Association: The Background to the Abortion of Garvey's Scheme for African Colonization." Journal of African History, Vol. 14, 1973, pp. 105 - 127.

The writer looks at the reasons why Liberia severed connections with Garvey and the UNIA. Beginning in May, 1920, Garvey sent an emissary to Liberia to negotiate for land for the immigrants from the US. However, funds were insufficient and suspicions grew and when Garvey's team arrived to erect buildings, they were seized, detained, and then deported. The Liberian government explained that they were not symphathizers with the Movement "which tends to intensify racial feelings of hatred and ill-will."

219. Alleyne, C. C. "The Menace of Garveyism." AME Zion Quarterly Review, Vol. 34, 1923, pp. 47 - 49.

This editorial described the UNIA as "Black Klu Kluxism" and Garvey as a "mistaken, misguided misanthrope." The editorial concludes that this Movement embodied "the greatest menace to the race today."

220. Bennett, Lerone Jr. "Marcus Garvey's Day of Triumph." Ebony, Vol. 32, November, 1976, pp. 168 - 178.

This day of triumph was Monday, August 2, 1920, when Garvey led a parade down Lenox Avenue through Harlem, New York. This was the greatest march that had ever occurred in that section of New York. The writer concludes that some 20 years after Garvey's death, in Africa and the Americas, Garvey's name was restored to its rightful place, high on the list of dreamers who worked in the wilderness to prepare the way for a Promised Land they were destined not to see.

221. ______. "Ghost of Marcus." Ebony, Vol. 15, March, 1960, pp. 53 - 58.

This article, mostly based upon interviews with Garvey's wife and former wife, discusses the impact of Garvey's Movement, its relevance, and the contemporary implications pointing out the rightness of Garvey's Movement. Amy Jacques Garvey talks of Garvey's ideals and her commitment to continue his work. Amy Ashwood, Garvey's first wife, also discusses Garvey's Movement and his conflict with the NAACP.

222. Briggs, Cyril. "The Decline of the Garvey Movement." Communist, Vol. 10, June, 1931, pp. 547 - 552.

The article begins with a discussion of conditions in America surrounding the beginning of the Garvey Movement. The author focuses upon the implementation of the Garvey Movement, the differences between the Garvey Movement and those aspects of other Black leaders of the time. Although crediting the Garvey Movement as a possible reactionary force, the author concludes that the Movement became subjective to the desires of the imperalists because of Garvey's mistakes.

223. ______. "Our Approach to The Garveyites." Vincent, Theodore G. and Chrisman, Robert, Editors. In Voices of A Black Nation: Political Journalism in The Harlem Renaissance, San Francisco: Ramparts Press, 1973.

The author notes that Blacks enlisted into the Garvey Movement as a way out of national oppression and degradation. These members were willing to fight to liberate Africa, the West Indies, and the Southern Black Belt, but Garvey's leadership proved to be politically weak, concludes Briggs.

224. Brisbane, Robert Hughes, Jr. "Some New Light on the Garvey Movement." Journal of Negro History, Vol. 1, January, 1951, pp. 53 - 62.

This article discusses Garvey's earlier life in the West Indies and London before his arrival in America. He cites reasons why Garvey was able to mobilize the masses of Blacks. He also places Garvey in the perspective of the "New Negro" or Negritude Movement. He credits Garveys as being one of the forerunners in soliciting racial pride in both Black and African concepts.

225. ______. "His Excellency: The Provincial President of Africa." Phylon, Vol. 10, 1949, pp. 257 - 265.

The article begins with a brief biographical sketch of Garvey. Discussion is given to Garvey's participation in protest movements in Jamaica and his travels to other West Indian islands, Central and South America and London. The article further extrapolates on his return to Jamaica and his founding theme of the Universal Negro Improvement Association and African Communities League. The article discusses Garvey's arrival in America and the founding of the UNIA. Discussion is also given to Garvey's opposition to the professional Negro leaders' attempts towards social equanamity in this country. The rise and fall of Garvey's Movement, its impact on literary creations during the 1920s, and its effect on integration of

Brisbane, Robert Hughes, Jr.

Blacks into American society.

226. Caldwell, William. "From Abraham Lincoln to Martin Luther King, Jr." Samtiden (Norway), Vol. 72, No. 10, 1963, pp. 669 - 680.

Marcus Garvey is included in this article. The author contends that Garvey elicited aspiration into Blacks in America with his emigration ideas and creation of an image of self-respect for Blacks.

227. Calvin, Floyd J. "The NAACP vs. The UNIA." Vincent, Theodore G. and Chrisman, Robert, Editors. Voices of A Black Nation: Political Journalism in the Harlem Renaissance, San Francisco: Ramparts Press, 1973.

The writer looks at the positive and the negative aspects of the NAACP and the UNIA. The NAACP denotes advancement and civil rights while the UNIA depicts improvement and racial pride. It was suggested that leaders of each organization proceed with the ideals of the respective programs without fighting among themselves.

228. ______. "The Straw that Broke the Camel's Back." Vincent, Theodore G. and Chrisman, Robert, Editors, In Voices of A Black Nation: Political Journalism in the Harlem Renaissance, San Francisco: Ramparts Press, 1973.

The writer suggests that the NAACP and the UNIA should preserve some ideals and destroy others in each respective program. The author felt that although the leader of the UNIA had made errors, the entire organization should not be destroyed because of it.

229. Chaka, Oba. "Marcus Garvey - The Father of Revolutionary Black Nationalism" Journal of Black Poetry, Vol. 1, 1970 - 1971, pp. 82 - 96.

The author notes that since Garvey gave Blacks' lives meaning and knowledge coupled with understanding of themselves, he is the "Father of the Black Nation." He realized that independent Black Organization was the method for implementing an independent African Nation. The writer lists the seven stages of Garveyism.

230. Chalk, Frank. "DuBois and Garvey Confront Liberia: Two Incidents of the Coolidge Years." Canadian Journal of African Studies, Vol. 1, November, 1967, pp. 135 - 142.

Although the philosophies of Garvey and DuBois were

worlds apart, they both were deeply engrossed into Liberian affairs. Garvey sought to establish a new capital for the Universal Negro Improvement Association. In return for land, the UNIA would raise funds for Liberia and establish a trade route. In 1924 the UNIA and Liberia severed their relationship after failure of the Black Star Line and financial fraud of the UNIA.

231. Clarke, John Henrik. "The Neglected Dimensions of the Harlem Renaissance." Black World, Vol. 20, November, 1970, pp. 118 - 121.

The author noted that during the literary period of the Harlem Renaissance, Garvey was using Harlem as a base for a large Mass Movement of Blacks. He was able to convey his passionate belief that Africa was the home of a great civilization which would soon be revived.

232. ______. "Marcus Garvey: The Harlem Years." Transition, (Accra), October - December, 1974, pp. 14 - 19.

The article discusses Garvey's Back to Africa Movement and its significance for Black people during the Harlem Renaissance.

233. ______. "The Caribbean Antecedents of Marcus Garvey." In Marcus Garvey and The Vision of Africa, NY: Vintage Books, 1974, pp. 14 - 28.

The writer argues that Garvey from a historical setting that evolved early in the Fifteenth Century. He discusses the history of the European involvement in Colonialism and the slave trade. It was against this tradition that Garvey emerged and erected the largest Black Mass Movement of this century.

234. ______. "The Impact of Marcus Garvey on the Harlem Renaissance." In Marcus Garvey and The Vision of Africa, NY: Vintage Books, 1974, pp. 180 - 188.

The writer feels that while the literary aspect of the Harlem Renaissance was unfolding, Garvey and his Universal Negro Improvement Association, using Harlem as his base of operation, built the largest mass movement among Black people that this century has ever seen. He asserts that the Garvey Movement began to fragment and decline concurrently with the end of the Harlem Renaissance. The author concludes that this era had a connotation that is generally missed by most people who write about it.

235. Domingo, W. A. and Owen, Chandler. "The Policy of The Messenger on West Indian and American Negroes: W. A. Domingo vs. Chandler Owen." The Messenger, Vol. 5 , March 5, 1923, pp. 639 - 645.

Mr. Domingo wrote The Messenger in protest that whenever they write about Marcus Garvey, the magazine always stressed his Jamaican nationality. Domingo felt this was unfair to condemn all Jamaicans because of Garvey.

236. DuBois, W. E. B. "Marcus Garvey." Crisis, Vol. 21, No. 2, December, 1920, pp. 58 - 60.

This article gives discussion to Garvey's early life in Jamaica, his visits to Europe, and the establishment of the Negro Improvement Society. He states the Objectives of the Society and Garvey's plans for the "Black Star Lines." The article further depicts a discussion of Garvey's character, whether or not his movement is honest, his leadership qualities, and determination, etc.

237. ______. "The Black Star Line." Crisis, Vol. 24, No. 5, September, 1922, pp. 210 - 214.

This article is devoted to discussion of Garvey's management of the Black Star Lines. DuBois credits Garvey's steamship ventures as being the foundation of his rise to popularity. DuBois further states the plan to unite Blacks by a line of steamships was Garvey's only original contribution to the race problem. Throughout the article DuBois questions Garvey's business acumen in managing the Black Star Lines.

238. ______. "The UNIA." Crisis, Vol. 25, No. 3, January, 1923, pp. 120 - 122.

This article entails the facts concerning the membership and finances of the UNIA. The financial report for the year ending July 31, 1922 is discussed.

239. ______. "Marcus Garvey." Crisis, Vol. 21, No. 6, January, 1921, pp. 112 - 115.

This article considers Garvey's industrial enterprise and the feasibility of his overall plans.

240. ______. "A Lunatic or A Traitor." Crisis, Vol. 28, May, 1924, pp. 8 - 9.

This editorial said that Garvey was the most dangerous enemy of the Black race in America and in the world. It stated that Garvey convicted himself, not only in his deeds, but in the way he acted in court. He was refused bail because of the threats and assaults

DuBois, W. E. B.

charged against his organization. It also felt that Garvey should be deported.

241. Edmonson, Locksley. "The Internationalization of Black Power: Historical and Contemporary Perspectives." Mawazo, Vol. 1, December, 1968, pp. 16 - 30.

The writer notes the evolution of Black emancipation strivings through the contributions of W. E. B. DuBois, Marcus Garvey, George Padmore, Martin Luther King, Jr., Frantz Fanon, Malcolm X, and Stokely Carmichael. It points out the historically important phenomenon of the linkage of ideas and the historical interrelationships of Pan-Negro and Pan-African aspirations.

242. Elkins, W. F. "The Influence of Marcus on Africa: A British Report of 1922." Science and Society, Vol. 32, Summer, 1968, pp. 321 - 323.

This communication from R. C. F. Maugham, British Consul-General in Dakar, Senegal to George Couzon, Principal Secretary of State of Foreign Affairs of Great Britain, gives some insight on how Garvey's Movement flourished especially in British West Africa. On the contrary, Garvey's newspaper, The Negro World, was banned in the Caribbean.

243. ______. "Suppression of the Negro World in the British West Indies." Science and Society, Vol. 35, Fall, 1971, pp. 344 - 347.

British rulers banned The Negro World in their colonies because they feared that the Black Nationalist preachings of Garvey might inflame their subjects in the Caribbean. This ban did not succeed because copies were smuggled in through Gustomala and Mexico. Garvey believed this suppression of The Negro World by White Colonial governments in Africa and the West Indies revealed the real meaning of their doctrine of Black racial inferiority.

244. ______. "Unrest Among the Negroes: A British Document of 1919." Science and Society, Vol. 32, Winter, 1968, pp. 66 - 79.

In October, 1919, the British Government sent a confidential report the State Department concerning American Negro unrest. Alarmed by color disturbances and the growth of racial consciousness, they banned Garvey's The Negro World, fearing that Afro-American radicals might inflame their subjects. The document, Unrest Among Negroes in included.

245. Elkins, W. F. "Marcus Garvey: The Negro World and the British Indies, 1919 - 1920." Science and Society, Vol. 36, No. 1, 1972, pp. 63 - 77.

This article focuses on the impact of Garvey upon Black workers of The British West Indies. The discussion is centered upon the use of Garvey's paper, The Negro World, in apprising Blacks of the oppressive conditions which existed. The article discusses the smuggling in of the paper to the island and opposition against it.

246. ______. "Black Power in the British West Indies: The Trinidad Longshoremen's Strike of 1919." Science and Society, Vol. 33, Winter, 1969, pp. 71 - 73.

The writer focuses upon the Trinidad Longshoremen's Strike of 1919 and credits it as being one of the earliest effusions of Black Nationalism. The article also credits Garvey's teachings as indirectly inspiring the strike, as many of his followers on the island were leaders of the Trinidad Workingmen's Association.

247. Elmes, A. F. "Garvey and Garveyism: An Estimate." Opportunity, Vol. 3, May, 1925, pp. 139 - 141.

The writer states that there can be no doubt that there was something to Garvey's Movement. He discusses Garvey's personality, ideals, the work of the UNIA, and the concepts, and meaning of Garveyism.

248. Essien-Udom, E. U. "Garvey and Garveyism." Chace, William M. and Collier, Peter, Editors. In Justice Denied: The Black Man in White America, NY: Harcourt, Brace and World, 1970.

The authors give a summary of the life and philosophies of Garvey, who depicted an ability to understand the feelings and plights of the Black masses. His organization, the UNIA, won support where other groups had failed. The writers conclude that the Movement never attracted many of the Black middle class nor the key Black intellectuals. Two of Garvey's speeches, "Speech Delivered at Madison Square Garden," and "An Appeal to The Conscience of The Black Race To See Itself," are included.

249. Fein, Charlotte Phillips. "Marcus Garvey: His Opinions About Africa." Journal of Negro Education, Vol. 33, No. 4, 1964, pp. 446 - 449.

This article explores the ideas and opinions about Africa expressed by Garvey. It credits Garvey as the Leader of The First Mass Movement of Afro-American Nationalism. The main themes of Garvey's writings

Fein, Charlotte Phillips.

and speeches as they, relate to Africa are analyzed. Discussion is also given to Garvey's theories with respect to their accuracy, his mode of expression, effectiveness, and historical significance.

250. Fierce, Mildred C. "Economic Aspects of the Marcus Garvey Movement." Black Scholar, Vol. 3, March/April, 1972, pp. 50 - 61.

The most overwhelming aspect of Garveyism was the unprecedented appeal Garvey had for the Black masses. This research attempts to objectively evaluate Garvey's ideas apart from his personality. Although Garvey made many errors, he espoused a Black philosophy, and showed that the Black masses were eager to respond with confidence and support to creative leadership.

251. Forbes, George W. "Marcus Garvey and His League of Nations." AMF Church Review, Vol. 37, 1921, p. 166.

The editor asked where in Africa it was that Garvey planned to put all the American Negroes whom he presumably was intending to transport there; he praised the wisdom of the majority of Negroes who rejected these "vagaries and obsessions of an alien who neither from a knowledge of our past history is able to understand our present status nor with the orderly reflection of a logical mind is able to sketch a plan for our future that would win credence anywhere outside of a mad house."

252. ______. "Garvey's Plight: The Pity Of It All." AMF Review, Vol. 40, 1973, p. 50.

The author discusses Garvey's conviction of mail fraud charges and concludes that "We never saw in his scheme anything other than errant charlatanism."

253. Fortune, T. Thomas. "A Man Without A Country." Vincent, Theodore G. and Chrisman, Robert, Editors, In Voices Of A Black Nation: Political Journalism In The Harlem Renaissance, San Francisco: Ramparts Press, 1973.

The writers note that in attempting to gain nationalism in Africa, one must not sacrafice social, civil, and economic values. The more one values opportunities, the more help one can give the UNIA in its program of race upbringing concludes Fortune.

254. Foster, William Z. "The Garvey Movement." Political Affairs, Vol. 33, February, 1954, pp. 15 - 23.

Excerpts from one chapter of Foster's new book,

Foster, William Z.

The Negro People in American History. It details the beginning of the UNIA, the "Back to Africa" slogan Garvey used to cultivate his plan of returning Blacks to Africa, his disastrous Black Star Line, which collapsed and was liquidated, the political decline of Garvey, and the effects of Garveyism on Negro Nationalism.

255. Frazier, E. Franklin. "The DuBois Program In The Present Crisis." Race, Vol. 1, Winter, 1935 - 1936, pp. 11 - 13.

Dr. Frazier looks at the economic, social, and cultural aspects of W. E. B. DuBois' program. Franklin felt that DuBois' racial program could not be taken seriously. DuBois criticized Garvey's attempt as a genuine racial movement. Garvey's Movement was too closely related to the ideologies of the ignorant of the Black masses. Franklin also felt that the dominant social and economic forces in American life were destroying the possibility of the development of Black Nationalism.

256. ______. "Garvey: A Mass Leader." Nation, Vol. 123, August 18, 1926, pp. 147 - 148.

Frazier discusses some of the ways in which Garvey was able to mobilize the masses of Blacks. Frazier compares Garvey's methodology and aims with those of other notable leaders and organizations. The article also discusses Garvey's instilling racial pride into the Black race.

257. Graves, John L. "The Social Ideas of Marcus Garvey." Journal of Negro Education, Vol. 31, Winter, 1962, pp. 65 - 74.

The writer analyzes some ideas relative to American solutions to the race problem. Garveyism is treated as an aspect of the broader problem of American Nationalism. He evaluates Garvey's social thoughts and appraises his qualifications as a leader.

258. "Garvey." Opportunity, Vol. 2, September, 1924, pp. 284 - 285.

Brief report of the opening parade of the Fourth Annual Convention of the Universal Negro Improvement Association. The article cites a quote from Garvey expressing his attitudes toward Black pride.

259. "Garvey Again." Time, Vol. 4, August 11, 1924, pp. 3 - 4.

"Garvey Again." Time.

Notes the opening of the Fourth Annual Convention of the UNIA. It was to be a 31 day celebration. Over 3,500 marched in the parade. Speakers urged Blacks to migrate to Africa and a new city was to laid out for them in Liberia called "The New Palestine." In the meantime, the federal government indicted Garvey on income tax evasion charges and the Liberian government said that none of the Garveyites could enter the Republic.

260. "Garvey and Anarchism." Messenger, Vol. 4, October, 1922, pp. 500 - 502.

The writer cites the Garvey Movement as anarchistic. He notes how this organization has resorted to violence in silencing those who criticize Garveyism.

261. "Garvey's Military Leader Gives Up His Post In Disgust Saying Recent Chief Respects No Man." New York Age, August, 1924, pp. 1 - 2.

Captain E. L. Gaines, Military Commander, African Legion quit in disgust after Garvey did not pay his salary during the previous four years. Garvey has wanted to use Gaines' salary five more years.

262. "Garvey Willing to Leave Country If Liberated." Journal and Guide, August 8, 1925, pp. 1 - 2.

Suffering from bronchial asthma, Garvey sent a 51 page petition to the government asking for a pardon and promised to leave the country if released. He attacked the NAACP and W. E. B. DuBois, several Black newspapers, and his first wife.

263. "Garvey's Third Convention Opened With Garish Parade." New York Age, August 5, 1922, pp. 1 - 2.

August 1 was the day of the parade of the UNIA. Garvey was dressed in a blue, gold, red, and white uniform. The Motto was, "Back to Africa."

264. Garvey, Amy J. "Marcus Garvey and Pan-Africanism." Black World, Vol. 21, December, 1971, pp. 15 - 18.

Mrs. Garvey notes that her husband believed in the redemption of Africa and envisioned Africa to be liberated from White leadership. She felt that the real test of his importance is that his philosophies have survived over the years. She points out that Garvey's body was transported to Jamaica in 1964 and was proclaimed Jamaica's National Hero.

265. Garvey, Amy J. "The Political Activities of Marcus Garvey in Jamaica." Jamaica Journal, June, 1972.

The writer asserts that Garvey and his colleagues formed a political party, "The Peoples' Political Party" in Jamaica in 1929 and issued a Manifesto. In the subsequent municipal elections, his party won three seats. The author concludes that the political and economic reforms that Garvey suggested in Jamaica set the pattern for all the other Caribbean territories.

266. ______. "The Early Years of Marcus Garvey," In Clarke, John Henrik, Marcus Garvey and The Vision of Africa, NY: Vintage Books, 1974, pp. 29 - 37.

The writer discusses Marcus Garvey from his birth in Jamaica in 1887 to his early days in Harlem, New York. She recalls his family, their backgrounds, and his travels from his country to England, and then to the United States. The author declares that Mr. Garvey started campaigning in Harlem as a soapbox speaker on street corners. His wife concludes that Garvey rallied people around him because he was talking about a positive international program, not just an anti-lynching protest. She concludes that he opposed integration of the races as racial suicide and an easy solution espoused by persons who did not have the courage and determination to keep on fighting for their civil rights to live and work as other racial groups did.

267. Grant, George S. "Garveyism and the Klu Klux Klan." Messenger, Vol. 15, October, 1923, pp. 835, 836, 842.

He cited the Garvey Movement and the Klu Klux Klan as teaching and encouraging racial hatred because of color, race, and religion by pitting group against group. Notice that all races must work concertedly, especially on the later force, to desist these cults.

268. Gray, Arthur S. "On Capitalism: I" Vincent, Theodore G. and Chrisman, Robert, Editors, In Voices Of A Black Nation: Political Journalism In The Harlem Renaissance, San Francisco: Ramparts Press, 1973.

The authors felt that even the most crudest form of communism was more beneficial to Black workers than any form of capitalism which condones lynchings, jim-crowism, and racial distinction.

269. "Gunning For The Negro Moses." Literary Digest, Vol. 74, August 19, 1921, pp. 40, 42, 45.

The Friends of Negro Freedom announced a series of

"Gunning For The Negro Moses." Literary Digest.

meetings to drive Garvey out of the country. There had been an article in The New York World on February 12, 1922 stating that $1,000,000 fraud had been connected to the Garvey Movement. The New York Tribune of July 10 told of Garvey's meeting with the Klu Klux Klan. W. E. B. DuBois in The Crisis wrote about the ill conceptions of the Garvey Movement. William Pickens of the NAACP had also forewarned of Garvey. Garvey retaliated with constant addresses haranguing his detractors in The Negro World in which he warned his followers of being led astray.

270. Harris, Abram L. "The Negro Problem As Viewed By Negro Leaders." Current History, Vol. 18, June, 1923, pp. 140 - 148.

This article discusses the different points of view among Black leaders during the 1920s on the question of interracial relations, the movement for industrial efficiency, the social equanimity issue, radical elements among younger Blacks, eminent Black scholars and intellectuals, and the meaning of Garveyism. Garvey is termed as not being a radical but a reactionary.

271. Hart, Richard. "The Life and Resurrection of Marcus Garvey." Race, Vol. IX, No. II, 1967, pp. 217 - 237.

This article begins with a discussion of the actions taken by the Jamaican people in honoring Garvey after his death. It discusses Garvey's early life and formative influences, his activities in the USA and Jamaica, his philosophies and teachings, and his impact and effect upon Blacks. Also included is one Appendix listing some of Garvey's writings and speeches and another Appendix which is Garvey's Election Manifesto for the General Election in Jamaica in 1930, which was published in The Black Man, January 2, 1930.

272. Hartt, Rollin Lynde. "Negro Moses and His Campaign To Lead The Black Millions Into Their Promised Land." Independent, Vol. 105, February 26, 1921, pp. 205 - 206, 218 - 219.

The author cites the Garvey Movement as not merely a Back to Africa Movement, or an Africa For The Africans' Movement. It was a Movement, however, to win respect and defend Black men in a White society. Also included are the words to a song decreed by The Declaration of Independence of The Negro Race, as the anthem of the Black Race. It was The Universal Ethiopian Anthem, by Burrell and Ford.

273. Haynes, Samuel A. "The Vision and Victory of Garvey." Vincent, Theodore G. and Chrisman, Robert, Editors. In Voices Of A Black Nation: Political Journalism In The Harlem Renaissance, San Francisco: Ramparts Press, 1973.

The authors state that most of Garvey's enemies feel that he was essentially right in the fundamentals of his program. Garvey demonstrated that Blacks could be organized and they were eager to support sincere Black leadership. Haynes concludes that the universality of his program brought Blacks together throughout the world.

274. Hill, Robert A. "The First England Years and After: 1912 - 1916." In Clarke, John Henrik, Marcus Garvey and The Vision of Africa, NY: Vintage Books, 1974, pp. 38 - 70.

The title tells what this article is about. He declares that Garvey's first encounter with English society was a gentle one. He states that Garvey attended Birkbeck College in England. Dr. Hill also discusses the individuals that Garvey met in London that were later to have profound impact upon his life.

275. "Huge Salary List of UNIA Disclosed When Men Are Fired." New York Age, August 12, 1922, pp. 1, 5.

Some high salaries officers were imprisoned from the Garvey Movement because of disloyalty to Garvey.

276. "Independents Name Tickets for Primary: Garveyite Named." New York Age, August 12, 1922, pp. 1 - 2.

Harlem Blacks named an independent candidate for Congress. "Sir" William H. Ferris of the UNIA - an independent ticket was proposed because of the strength of the Black vote in the Second District.

277. "Is Garveyism The Answer To The Present Problem Of The American Negro?" The American Negro, Vol. 1, August, 1955, pp. 19 - 23.

Biographical sketch and discussion by Naomi Williams Taylor and Theodore Silver. Ms. Taylor, who was Secretary General of the UNIA, felt that Garveyism was the answer. She felt that the only way Blacks would be respected by other races was through acceptance of Garveyism which taught racial pride, love, and racial consciousness. On the other hand, Silver felt that Blacks should not return to Africa but stay in America and fight oppression.

278. James, C. L. R. "Marcus Garvey." Black Lines, Vol. 1, No. 3, Spring, 1971, pp. 8 - 12.

The writer contends that Garvey made the American Negro conscious of his African origin and created, for the first time, a feeling of international solidarity among Africans and people of African descent. Insofar as this is directed against oppression, surmises James, it is a progressive step. His Movement was, in many respects, absurd and in others thoroughly dishonest. Yet, the Garvey Movement, like the ICU, in the best days, though it actually achieved importance in the history of Negro revolts. The author concludes that the Garvey Movement shows the fires that smoulder in the Negro world, in America, as it does in Africa.

279. Johnson, Charles S. "After Garvey - What?" Opportunity, Vol. 1, August, 1923, pp. 231 - 233.

This article begins with a brief discussion of Garvey's conviction by the US government. It discusses Garvey's Movement as having been "The New Psychology Of The American Negro Peasantry." It depicts Garvey's Movement as being one of pure blooded Negroes.

280. Karioki, James N. "Pan-Africanism As An Evolving Concept." Black Lines, Vol. 1, Spring, 1971, pp. 5 - 7.

The writer cites C. L. R. James' analysis of the Garvey Movement during the 1920s, concluding that although Garveyism had no specific program, the Movement was instrumental in kindling the awareness of the common destiny of Black people.

281. Langley, Jabez Ayodele. "Garveyism and African Nationalism." Race, Vol. 11, October, 1969, pp. 157 - 160, 163 - 165, 160 - 170.

The writer looks at the influence of Garveyism on African Nationalism,and concluded that the Movement had no permanent influence since Africans felt that Africa must be controlled and directed from "African Africa and thoroughly African Africans."

282. Lewis, Rupert. "The Last London Years: 1935 - 1940." In Clarke, John Henrik, Marcus Garvey and The Vision Of Africa, NY: Vintage Books, 1974, pp. 330 - 341.

The title tells what this article is about. While in London, Garvey reestablished the headquarters of the UNIA. The writer concludes that during those last London years, Garvey never departed from the principles which guided his historical task. Neither imprisonment, betrayal, nor financial deprivation could

Lewis, Rupert.

deter his activities or lead him to despondency as he saw the forward movement of Colonial people gaining momentum against Imperialism, concludes Lewis.

283. "Marcus Garvey." Messenger, Vol. 4, June, 1922, pp. 417 - 418.

Justice Panken of the Seventh District Court severely rebuked Garvey when it was learned that most of the $600,000 invested in the Black Star Line by poor Blacks was practically gone. Justice Panken told Garvey that he had preyed upon the gullibility of his own people and that he should have built a hospital with the money. It was noted that The Messenger has warned the people of this doomed project.

284. "Marcus Garvey." Journal of Negro History, Vol. 25, October, 1940, pp. 590 - 592.

This short biographical sketch noted that Garvey's claim to history was the fact that he attracted a larger following than any other Black leader in modern times. His impact was felt worldwide. It also notes that Blacks of today owe their prominence to White men who used them as a means to keep the Black man in his place. Marcus Garvey died in London on June 10, 1940.

285. "Marcus Garvey and Three Others Indicted by Federal Grand Jury." New York Age, February 25, 1922, pp. 1, 7.

On February 16, the Federal Grand Jury indicted Marcus Garvey, Elie Garcia, George Tobias, and Orlando M. Thompson on mail fraud charges.

286. "Marcus Garvey Excoriates Race Down In North Carolina." New York Age, November 11, 1922, pp. 1 - 2.

Speaking at the North Carolina State Fair, Garvey said that the Black man had to be beaten and lynched before he became race conscious. He thanked the White man for this maltreatment and said that in Africa the Whites would be despised by the ruling Black Race.

287. "Marcus Garvey Hopes To Prevent Deportation." New York Amsterdam News, November 30, 1927, pp. 1, 4.

It was announced that Garvey, in jail for mail fraud, would be deported to Jamaica. After leaving prison, Garvey went to New Orleans to fight his deportation.

288. "Marcus Garvey Is Wed In Baltimore." New York Age, August 5, 1922, pp. 1 - 2.

Marcus Garvey and his Secretary, Amy Jacques, were married in Baltimore on July 27, 1922.

289. "Marcus Garvey Now In Atlanta Prison." New York Age, February 14, 1925, pp. 1 - 2.

Garvey began serving a 95 year prison sentence. His followers vowed to await his return and adhere to his causes. Thousands were at the Tombs Prison in New York to see him depart for the federal prison in Atlanta.

290. "Marcus Garvey to William Pickens and William Pickens to Marcus Garvey." Messenger, Vol. 4, August, 1922, pp. 471 - 472.

Shows two letters written in July, 1922. The first is from Garvey to Professor William Pickens inviting him to attend the Third Annual International Convention of The Negro Peoples Of The World. The second letter was Pickens' response in which he refused to be honored by organizations friendly to the Klu Klux Klan or the Black Hand Society.

291. "Marcus Garvey - The Garvey Movement: A Promise Or A Menace to Negroes?" Messenger, Vol. 2, October, 1920, pp. 114 - 115.

The writer looks at the political aspects of the Garvey Movement which has proposed a Negro Party. This editorial expressed the view that this would not work because minority groups can never become majority groups and since most Blacks do not vote, the party would be pursuing a political doctrine of "impossibility." The party could never secure legislation for the sole benefit of Blacks, contends the editor.

292. Martin, Tony. "C. L. R. James and the Race/Class Question." Race, October, 1972, Vol. 14, pp. 183 - 193.

In the struggle of Blacks for liberation from Colonalism and racial prejudice, the race/class question exists. People like Garvey argued for the primacy of race and emphasized the Black Nationalism aspect of the struggle. Others like Black Communists, advocated the primacy of class struggle, concludes Martin.

293. Matthews, Mark D. "His Philosophy and Opinions: Perspective On Marcus Garvey." Black World, February, 1976, pp. 36 - 53.

Matthews, Mark D.

This article makes an analysis of the philosophies and opinions of Garvey. The writer asserts that Garvey was a staunch Materialist as well as an ardent Nationalist. A materialist in the sense of his analysis of phenomenon started from the material conditions instead of idealism.

294. Miller, Kelly. "After Marcus Garvey - What of Negroes?" Contemporary Review, (NY), Vol. 131, April, 1927, pp. 492 - 495.

This article begins with a biographical sketch of Garvey, the early formulation of his ideas, and the development of his Movement. Discussion is given to the forming of the UNIA and the publishing of The Negro World. Considerable discussion is given to Garvey's opposition from the Black Intelligentsia and his association with the Klu Klux Klan. The overall impact of Garvey's Movement is discussed.

295. Minor, Robert. "Death Or A Program!" Workers' Monthly, Vol. 5, April, 1926, pp. 270 - 273, 281.

This article discusses the pros and cons of Garvey and the UNIA. The writer discusses the future of the Garvey Movement since the incarceration of its leader. He raises the question, "Should It Be Saved Or Destroyed?" Some believed that the Garvey Movement was a menace, while others believed it was necessary.

296. Moore, Richard B. "The Critics and Opponents of Marcus Garvey." In Clarke, John Henrik, Marcus Garvey and The Vision Of Africa, NY: Vintage Books, 1974, pp. 210 - 235.

The writer argues that to fully understand Garvey's critics due consideration must be given to such opposition in any historical study of the man and the Movement which he led if such a study is to be adequate and comprehensive. He concludes that an account of this opposition seems particularly relevant and required when it is realized that such opposition may have played an important role in hastening the decline of this Mass Movement and its rapid reduction to a number of ineffective splinter groups.

297. "Mr. Bilbo's Afflatus." Time, Vol. 33, May 8, 1939, pp. 14 - 15.

Theodore Bilbo read a petition in Congress which bore 2,500,000 names of Blacks who wanted to live in Africa. He wanted the government to establish a Greater Liberia for "repartriated" Blacks. He said that the US could

"Mr. Bilbo's Afflatus." Time.

rid itself of a depressed and depressing race and save itself from racial "amalgamation." Also backing the bill was Mittie Gordon who had gotten petitions by her Peace Movement of Ethiopia. She was a follower of Garvey and members of the existing UNIA affiliates backed the bill. Opposition to the bill came from the NAACP and other Black leaders who charged that Bilbo muzzled Black workers in his pecan grove.

298. "Negro Deputy of France Condemns Garvey." Messenger, Vol. 4, December, 1922, pp. 538 - 539.

Monsieur Diagne, Senegalese Deputy, denounced Garvey by saying, "Garvey's crusade for the redemption of Africa can only fall flat, for Africa's Negroes are diverse and lacking in cohesion. The dangerous utopia proposed would not serve their real interest."

299. "Negro Exodus Unnecessary." Opportunity, Vol. 2, October, 1924, pp. 312 - 313.

This article attempts to show reasons why Garvey's attempt at colonizing Black Americans in Africa was having "little success" as of October, 1924. The writer expressed that the Black American in 1924 was making too much "progress" to even consider leaving America.

300. "Negro Leadership in America." World's Work, Vol. 41, March, 1921, pp. 435 - 436.

A copy of a letter sent by Rev. C. S. Smith, Bishop of The AME Church, which takes exception to an editorial note in December, 1920 World's Work. It accompanied an article about Garvey by Truman Talley and it said that Garvey was the best point in which to study what is going on in the heads of ten million Blacks. Rev. Smith felt that Garvey did not interpret the thoughts of one percent of the Black Race. He also felt that Garvey's aim to send Blacks to Liberia was unsound and referred the readers to consult the American Consul-General for Liberia, Dr. Ernest Lyon, for confirmation of this point.

301. "New Orleans Women - Garvey Followers, Stir City By Letter." New York Age, March 10, 1023, pp. 1 - 2.

A group of women, "The Voluntary Committee of the UNIA," sent a letter to the mayor asking for relief from police surveilance during meetings. A copy of the letter is shown.

302. "No Bail Yet For Garvey." New York Amsterdam News, June 27, 1923, pp. 1, 2.

Federal Judge refused to grant bail to Garvey pending an appeal of his conviction for mail fraud. Garvey's lawyer considered going to the Supreme Court to secure his release. It was felt that Garvey would flee the country if released.

303. O'Neal, James. "The Next Emancipation." Messenger, Vol. 4, September, 1923, pp. 481 - 482.

The author commenting on Garvey's idea to create a Black Africa that would be ruled by Blacks felt that if Garvey did expel Whites from Africa, he would establish Black Capitalism instead of the existing White Capitalism there. He would only change the color of the exploiters. The writer suggests that Blacks stay in America and join White workers in abolishing Capitalism.

304. Owen, Chandler. "Should Marcus Garvey Be Deported?" Messenger, Vol. 4, September, 1922, pp. 479 - 480.

The Friends of Negro Freedom urged an early trial for Garvey and convictions of all eight charges against him. Since Garvey had swindled his own people, had become a friend of the Klu Klux Klan, and had disgraced his race by his comical tactics, the organization proposed that "Marcus Garvey Must Go" Campaign be formed.

305. Padmore, George. "The Bankruptcy of Negro Leadership." Vincent, Theodore G. and Chrisman, Robert, Editors. In Voices Of A Black Nation: Political Journalism In The Harlem Renaissance, San Francisco: Ramparts Press, 1973.

The writer talks about how so-called Black leaders were betraying Blacks. He cites such leaders as Oscar dePriest, W. E. B. DuBois, and Major R. R. Morton as some examples. Padmore felt that the chief offender was Garvey who had exploited the racial consciousness of Blacks. He felt that Garvey was trying to dupe Blacks into believing that if they supported his financially, he could compel the League of Nations to free Africa.

306. ______. "Garveyism in The West Indies." Vincent, Theodore G. and Chrisman, Robert, Editors. In Voices Of A Black Nation: Political Journalism In The Harlem Renaissance, San Francisco: Ramparts Press, 1973.

Padmore notes correspondence between Henry H. Kendal and himself. Kendal was concerned about the criticisms of Garvey in the Negro Worker and felt that it

Padmore, George.

should stop. Padmore replied that they would continue to expose the schemes of Garvey who had done nothing to help workers to gain benefits or to unionize. Padmore felt that Garvey's "radical" talk allowed him to fool the Black masses.

307. ______. "On Capitalism: 2." Vincent, Theodore G. and Chrisman, Robert, Editors. In Voices Of A Black Nation: Political Journalism In The Harlem Renaissance, San Francisco: Ramparts Press, 1973.

An attack on Arthur S. Gray's support of Marcus Garvey. Gray had previously said that communism was more beneficial to Black workers than capitalism. Yet, he supported a man who swindled the oppressed, states Padmore. He stressed the need for all workers to strive for unity of all oppressed people through a program of militant class struggles, represented by the International Trade Union Committee of Negro Workers.

308. Pickens, William. "Africa for the African: The Garvey Movement." Nation, Vol. 113, December 28, 1921, pp. 750 - 751.

This article discussed the Garvey Movement by posing such questions as: Whether or not a Republic of Africa, controlled by Blacks is possible? The article also discussed Garvey's emphasis on racial consciousness, the weaknesses of his business acumen and methodology, the effects of his Movement on the domestic struggle in America, and possible color division among Black Americans that the Movement may create.

309. ______. "The Emperor of Africa: The Psychology of Garveyism." Forum, Vol. LXX, August, 1923, pp. 1709 - 1799.

This article focuses upon the rise and demise of Garvey and his Movement. It discusses his plans for a Pan-African Kindom-Republic and to the ways in which Garvey was able to mobilize the masses of Blacks. Discussion is also given to Garvey's relationship with the Klu Klux Klan.

310. _____. "Marcus Garvey." New Republic, Vol. LII, August 31, 1973, pp. 46 - 47.

An open letter printed in The New Republic discusses the issues surrounding the imprisonment of Garvey. It is the writer's contention that no useful purpose was being served by the continued imprisonment of Garvey.

311. "Potentate of UNIA Ordered Arrested and Sent to Atlanta." New York Amsterdam News, February 4, 1925, pp. 1 - 2.

The conviction of Marcus Garvey was upheld and he was ordered arrested and sent to Atlanta to begin his sentence. Judge Mack said the jury was justified in the sentence because the company was in bad condition and Garvey led people to put their money in a worthless business. His first wife was also suing him for a divorce.

312. "Prosecution Rests In Garvey's Case." Journal and Guide, June 9, 1923, pp. 1, 4.

The treasurer of the Black Star Line testified that Garvey had control of all money gotten from the sale of stocks and used it as he wished. Counsel for the North American Steamship Company testified that Garvey wanted only Liberian officers for his ship, plus Garvey did not have money to have the registry changed or for insurance for the ship.

313. Randolph, A. Philip. "Garveyism." Messenger, Vol. 3, September, 1921, pp. 248 - 252.

The writer cites Garveyism as "a natural and logical reaction of Black Men to the overwhelming and supercilious conduct of White Imperalists." Randolph felt that Garvey's "Africa For The Africans" Movement was not the immediate program for Blacks in light of modern world politics. Randolph concludes that Garvey's program widens the hostility between Black and White workers and could only lead to further racial riots.

314. ______. "Black Zionism." Messenger, Vol. 4, January, 1922, pp. 330 - 331, 334 - 335.

Randolph felt that Garveyism would not liberate Africa. It would only regress the progress by repeling Blacks from the prolatarian liberation movement, political and economic efforts of solidarity, class-consciousness, thus pitting them against the White workers' struggle for liberation.

315. ______. "Reply to Marcus Garvey." Messenger, Vol. 4, August, 1922, pp. 467 - 471.

Randolph addressed himself to the accusations made by Garvey in the Negro World against The Messenger. Garvey stated that The Messenger was published irregularly and questioned the business acumen of Randolph and Chandler Owen. The article goes on to tell of what Randolph and Owen have and have not done for the Black Race. Randolph states that Garvey should be deported.

316. Randolph, A. Philip. "The Human Hand Treat." Messenger, Vol. 4, October, 1922, pp. 499 - 500.

Randolph related his experience of receiving a package in the mail which contained a human hand and a threatening letter instructing him to join Garvey's "nigger improvement assocation." The letter was from the Ku Klux Klan. The Klan had selected Garvey as the model of Black leadership.

317. Ransom, Reverdy Cassius. "Back to Africa: A Militant Call." AME Church Review, Vol. 37, 1920, p. 88.

The editor comments on the contents of the UNIA's Declaration of Rights. He characterized it as a welcome document, calculated to rouse Black people around the world "to preserve their national and territorial inheritance in Africa, and to take a place of racial respect and independence among the free and liberty-loving people of the world."

318. ______. "A Quadrilateral View of the Attitude and Outlook for Negroes Throughout the World." AME Church Review, Vol. 38, 1921, pp. 82 - 85.

The writer discusses Garvey and other leaders on the merits of the recent Pan-African Congress held in Paris. Garvey was bitterly opposed to the W. E. B. DuBois - sponsored Paris meeting.

319. ______. "The Golden Dream of Negro Nationality." AME Church Review, Vol. 40, 1923, p. 44.

The author accepted the Negro World's analogy comparing Garvey favorably to Denmark Vesey and observed that "It is not often that a prophet appears among the people of any race." Ransom agreed with Garvey's Back to Africa plan.

320. ______. "Marcus Garvey: Mightiest Prophet." Pittsburgh Courier, December 17, 1927, p. 4.

The bishop declares that as a prophet, Garvey has run true to form by meeting the age-long rewards of the prophets - he has been stoned, imprisoned, and how he has been banished. But truth, aspirations, and ideals can neither be imprisoned nor deported.

321. Reed, Beverley. "Amy Jacques Garvey: Black, Beautiful, and Free." Ebony, July, 1971, pp. 45 - 54.

Widow of Garvey carries on his work from her Jamaican home by corresponding with scholars and professors world-wide and doing research and documentation for them. She states that Garvey's grand plan never materialized because of his enemies. The wife of the

Reed, Beverley.

leader feels that W. E. B. DuBois was the one most responsible for the failure of the plan; she claims that Marcus Garvey was the first to say "Black Is Beautiful."

322. Roger, Benjamin F. "William E. B. DuBois, Marcus Garvey, and Pan-Africa." Journal of Negro History, Vol. 40, No. 2, 1955, pp. 154 - 165.

This article begins by describing the conditions facing Blacks after the first World War: race riots, lynchings, the power of the Klan, and the need for Black leaders. It discusses the role of DuBois and Garvey in providing that leadership during the 1920s. The article discusses the two leaders.

323. Rudwick, Elliott M. "DuBois Versus Garvey: Race Propagandists At War." Journal of Negro Education, Vol. 28, Fall, 1959, pp. 421 - 429.

The author notes that W. E. B. DuBois and Marcus Garvey clashed in their separate plans to establish an African state and an international organization of Negroes. Unlike DuBois, Garvey was able to establish mass support and his program had a tremendous emotional appeal. During the 1920s, in their newspapers, The Crisis and Negro World, they attacked each other. The author concludes that Garvey was explosive, irrational, and flamboyant, which attracted frustrated, uneducated Blacks. DuBois was moderate, thoughtful, and analytical which appealed to a minority within a minority.

333. "Seligman Interviews Garvey and Writes His Impressions." New York Age, December 10, 1921, pp. 1 - 2.

Herbert Seligman of the NAACP talked with Marcus Garvey and felt that although he had faith in himself, Garvey's ventures were neither realistic nor sound.

334. Shepperson, George. "Notes on Negro American Influences on the Emergence of African Nationalism." Journal of African History, Vol. 1, No. 2, 1960, pp. 299 - 312.

This article discusses the impact and influence of three Black West Indians: Edward Blyden, Marcus Garvey, and George Padmore, upon Black Americans' interests in and influences on Africa. The article also gives a brief biographical sketch of each individual.

335. Shepperson, George. "Pan Africanism and 'Pan-Afarican-ism:' Some Historical Notes." Phylon, Vol. 23, No. 4, 1962, pp. 346 - 358.

The writer looks at Garvey's role in the Pan-African Movement. Shepperson noted that when the Pan-African Movement was in the hands of American Blacks, Garveyism was an embarassment to them, but when Africans took over, it became an almost essential element.

336. Simmons, C. W. "Negro Intellectuals' Criticism of Garveyism." Negro History Bulletin, Vol. 25, November, 1961, pp. 33 - 35.

This article surveys the views and opinions of such Black intellectuals as DuBois, A. Philip Randolph, Alain Locke, E. Franklin Frazier, and James Weldon Johnson, toward Garvey and his Movement.

337. "Six Thousand Garveyites Hear Their Leader: On Bail From Prison." New York Age, September 22, 1923. p. 1.

Garvey made his first appearance at a UNIA meeting on September 13. He had been imprisoned since June 18 and was out on bail.

338. "Six Thousand Dollar Salary Not Enough for Dr. Bundy." New York Age, September 23, 1922, pp. 1, 5.

After salaries of the UNIA's officials were reduced, Dr. Leroy Bundy said he could not live on his $500 a month salary.

339. "Sketch of Marcus Garvey." Journal of Negro History, Vol. 25, 1940, pp. 590 - 592.

Short biographical sketch of Garvey written immediately after his death. Discussion given to opposition to Garvey's Movement and events surrounding Garvey's failure and imprisonment.

340. Slocum, William J. "Sucker Traps: Plain and Fancy." Collier's, Vol. CXXV, January 28, 1950, pp. 49 - 50.

This article focuses on the work of the Post Office Inspection Service on cracking down on con schemes handled through the mail. Article credits the post office with interrupting notion of "fabulous common career of self-appointed Admiral Marcus Aurelius Garvey." It focuses on events surrounding Garvey's arrest and conviction of fraud through the use of the mail.

341. Starling, Lathan, Sr. and Franklin, Donald. "The Life and Work of Marcus Garvey." Negro History Bulletin, Vol. 26, No. 1, 1962 - 1963, pp. 36 - 38.

This article discusses Garvey's impact upon Black Americans in instilling racial consciousness and pride. Garvey's life and his involvement with the Black Movement are discussed. The author also devoted considerable amount of discussion to the meaning of Garveyism and comments on it.

342. "Steps From Behind Prison Bars In $15,000 Cash Bail Pending Appeal." New York Amsterdam News, September 12, 1923, pp. 1, 2.

After almost three months in prison, Garvey was released on bond. A cash bond of $15,000 was put up for his release which was raised by the UNIA. Only a few of Garvey's followers were at the prison when he was released.

343. Streator, George. "In Search of Leadership." Race, Vol. 1, Winter, 1935 - 1936, pp. 14 - 20.

It was Garvey who apprised Blacks of their kinship with the Blacks in Africa. Garvey's dream was one of a Black Imperialism which would inspire Black men to migrate to Africa. The writer concludes that The Garvey Movement and others,on different scales and levels, were symptomatic of the development of racial consciousness as a means of solving the economic problems of the peoples of African descent in America.

344. ______. "Three Men: Napier, Morton, Garvey - Negro Leaders Who Typified An Era for Their People." Commonwealth, Vol. 32, August 9, 1940, pp. 323 - 326.

This article gives brief biographical sketches of James Napier, a Black banker and businessman, Booker T. Washington as President of Tuskegee Institute in 1915, and Marcus Garvey, Founder and Organizer of the United Negro Improvement Association.

345. Talley, Truman Hughes. "Garvey's Empire of Ethiopia" World's Work, Vol. 41, January, 1921, pp. 264 - 270.

This article deals with Garvey's influencing the change of attitudes of Black Americans in their views toward Whites and their own destinies. Discussion of Garvey's plans of achieving Black independence also.

346. ______. "Marcus Garvey: The Negro Moses?" World's Work, Vol. 41, December, 1920, pp. 153 - 166.

Talley, Truman Hughes.

Article is a discussion of Garvey's personal history and further extrapolates on his ideas and the oppositions to Garvey's Movement. The article focuses on the impact of Garvey on the minds and attitudes of Black Americans.

347. "The Influence of Marcus Garvey on Africa: A British Report of 1922." Science and Society, Summer, 1968, pp. 321 - 323.

Reprint of a communication from R. C. F. Maughen, British Consul-General in Dakar, Senegal, to George Curzon, Principal Secretary of State for Foreign Affairs of Great Britain. Discusses the dissemination of Garvey's ideas in British West Africa.

348. Tolbert, Emory. "Outpost Garveyism and The UNIA: Rank and File." Journal of Black Studies, Vol. 5, March, 1975, pp. 233 - 253.

The author depicts the Los Angeles Chapter of the UNIA. He examines how they interpreted Garveyism, the regional, and historical context associated with the arrival of the UNIA to Los Angeles, the early social composition of the Los Angeles rank and file, and how they differed from their local competitor, the NAACP.

349. ______. "The Garvey Movement." Opportunity, Vol. 4, November, 1926, pp. 346 - 348.

This article depicts a discussion of the circumstances surrounding Garvey's arrest and attempts to retrace Garvey's Movement and the fulfillment of his ideas and promises. The article credits Garvey's success to his ability to mobilize the masses. The article concludes that with the evidence available, Garvey cannot be classified as a swindler, but rather he failed to deal realistically with life.

350. Tuttle, Worth M. "Garveyism" Impressions From A Missionary School." World Tomorrow, Vol. 4, June, 1921, pp. 183 - 184.

At a missionary school in the far South, a speaker was brought in to discuss the growing racial consciousness. There were five distinct attitudes toward Garveyism at school. They felt that although his plan was weak, they supported his ideas. They thrilled at the thought of a future nationality. They had developed racial pride. They also were friendly toward White faculty who had an interest in racial consciousness. They saw the possibility of racial conflict if Whites attempted to destroy Garveyism.

351. Tuttle, Worth M. "A New Nation in Harlem." World Tomorrow, Vol. 4, September, 1921, pp. 279 - 281.

A discussion of the UNIA meetings in Harlem, New York. This particular article deals specifically with the Second International Convention of the UNIA that was held at Liberty Hall in Harlem in 1921. The author attended this convention and gives a detailed account of the conferences.

352. Waldron, Eric D. "Imperator Africans - Marcus Garvey: Menace or Promise?" Independent, Vol. CXIV, January 3, 1925, pp. 8 - 11.

The article begins discussing the Garvey Movement by focusing upon the conditions and attitudes of Black Americans after the war. The article then proceeds to discuss Garvey's methods and ideals for instilling Black pride, the formation of the UNIA, and the Black Star Line. The article also discusses the failure of the Black Star Line and decline of Garvey's Movement. Opposition posed by other Black leaders is discussed.

353. Watkins, Ralph. "The Marcus Garvey Movement in Buffalo, New York." Afro-American in New York Life and History, Vol. 1, No. 1, January, 1977, pp. 37 - 48.

This article discusses the conflict between Garvey and some of Buffalo's Black ministers. The author concludes that the conflict was the result of their desire to maintain control over the direction of their community as opposed to Garvey's methodology of organization. This confrontation was not brought about by deeply seated ideological differences, states Watkins, because, in essence, both sides accepted the ideas that before the race could advance it had to be unified. The writer points out that the nucleus of the Garvey Movement in Buffalo, included the business and professional class as well as working class.

354. Weisbord, Robert G. "The Back-To-Africa Idea." History Today, (Great Britain), Vol. 18, No. 1, 1968, pp. 30 - 37.

This article focuses primarily upon movements concerning the idea of Blacks returning to Africa. Although the central theme focuses on Garvey's Movement, a considerable amount of discussion is given to the American Colonization Society, the settlement of Liberia by Blacks, and the role of Martin R. Delaney. The article also discusses Garvey's influence on Blacks wishing to return to Africa and the opposition Garvey faced from DuBois and the NAACP.

355. Weisbord, Robert G. "Marcus Garvey - Pan-Negroist: The View From Whitehall." Race, Vol. 2, No. 2, April, 1970, pp. 419, 427 - 428.

The writer points out that more than any other Black leader, the charismatic Garvey in his worldwide activities underlined the international character of the color problem. He was a Pan-Negroist without equal. Weisbord surmises that today (1970) in England itself, Garvey is lauded, even defied by Black Power advocates from the West Indies and Africa. The author concludes that in a very real sense, as far as the British Empire is concerned, Garveyism has triumphed. Whitehall had good reason to be worried, states the writer.

6
GENERAL ARTICLES

356. "A Black Aaron Burr." Time, Vol. 1, June 11, 1923, p. 4.

The prosecution rested its case against Marcus Garvey in mail fraud charges stemming from the selling of stocks of the Black Star Line. This article details his plan to get Blacks to migrate to Africa.

357. "Acting Heads Of UNIA To Be Named At Meeting." New York Age, August 17, 1940, p. 1.

An emergency conference was convened for late August to select acting heads and other officers of the UNIA.

358. "African Colonization Schemes." New York Age, August 12, 1922, p. 4.

The editor talks about African colonizations of Marcus Garvey and Dr. J. Albert Thomas. He felt that Blacks could do Africans more good by achieving full American citizen rights.

359. African Studies of The West Indies. "A Summary of The International Seminar On Marcus Garvey." Black Scholar, Vol. 4, February, 1973, pp. 58 - 60.

This seminar was a reevaluation of the present day state of research on Garvey and Garveyism and showed the resurgence of interest in Garvey in both the USA and abroad. Garvey's wife and son both spoke at the seminar. Some topics of discussion were: "The Impact of Marcus Garvey in Nigeria," "The Garvey Movement in California," "Marcus Garvey, The Negro World, and The British West Indies: 1919 -

African Studies of The West Indies.

1920," "Garvey and Trinidad," and "Marcus Garvey, Brake or Spur On African Nationalism," to name just a few.

360. "A Letter From Marcus Garvey." Crusader, Vol. 21, April, 1920, p. 5.

In response to the article in the March issue of The Crusader, on "A Paramount Chief of The Negro Race," Garvey wrote to say that it was the most intelligent explanation of the real purpose of the UNIA Convention. It was noted that Garvey missed the point - for the purpose of the article was to warn the people of the danger of electing a person to preside over the destiny of the Black Race.

361. "Amy Garvey Penniless, She Says." New York Amsterdam News, July 29, 1925, p. 1.

Garvey's first wife said she was in need of financial aid. She said she would sanction commuting Garvey's sentence, but she also said that it was ludicrous that such a man as Garvey would attempt to lead a race of people.

362. "A Negro Almost As Low As Garvey." Messenger, Vol. 4, November, 1922, p. 519.

It was noted that Rev. T. H. M. Gibson of the Calvalry Baptist Church in Indianapolis had a member of the Ku Klux Klan speak at the church and accepted a donation from the Klan. This action was interpreted by The Messenger as meaning that the minister and his church were members of the Garvey Movement.

363. "Anglo-Saxon Clubs and UNIA Form Working League." Journal and Guide, July 18, 1925, p. 1.

The Anglo-Saxon Clubs of America joined with the UNIA in combating the NAACP. It was felt that Garvey had pledged his support to an organization which humiliates and degrades the Black Race.

364. "Another Challenge to Garvey's Propaganda." New York Age, June 4, 1921, p. 1.

C. S. Smith offered $1,000 if anyone could prove that the Black Star Line was operating.

365. "Are We the Most Corrupt People?" Journal and Guide, October 6, 1923, p. 10.

Since his release on bail, Garvey had been claiming that Blacks had led his downfall. This editorial

"Are We the Most Corrupt People?"

felt that Garvey was the cause of his own problems and a leader who does not believe in those he leads, cannot believe in himself.

366. "A Supreme Negro Jamaican Jackass." Messenger, Vol. 5, January, 1923, p. 561.

The author notes that Garvey was playing the role of Monumental Monkey, the Southern White man's "good nigger," clown, and imperial buffon. It made reference to his statement in North Carolina in which he said that if he had to depend on Blacks to get him there he would have been walking six months. It was noted that it was money from Blacks, which he collected in the pretense of building a ship line, that spiraled him to fame.

367. "Atlanta Federal Prison Swings Open to Garvey Early Sunday Morning." Journal & Guide, February 14, 1925, pp. 1, 3.

Garvey entered the federal prison at Atlanta to begin his sentence. It was speculated that he would be deported.

368. Bagnall, Robert W. "The Madness of Marcus Garvey." Messenger, Vol. 5, March, 1923, pp. 638, 648.

The author was a critic of Garvey and an official of the NAACP. The writer states that there is much reason to believe that if Garvey were examined by alienists, he would be pronounced insane - a paranoiac. He surmises that if he were not insane, he was a demogogic charlatan, but the probability was that he was insane. Bagnall concludes that certainly the Movement was insane, whether Garvey was or not.

369. "Bail for Garvey." New York Amsterdam News, August 1, 1923, p. 12.

This editorial was of the opinion that Garvey himself was the main reason the judge denied bail. His actions during the trial may have been a deciding factor in being denied bail. Also, Garvey is not a citizen, and this may also account for his denial.

370. "Bail for Marcus Garvey." New York Amsterdam News, August 1, 1923, p. 12.

In this letter to the editor, Rev. E. Ethelred Brown wrote protesting the denial of bail to Garvey. He felt that this was unnecessary and unjustifiable discrimination against Garvey since even some murderers had previously been released pending sentencing.

371. "Black Cross Ship Arrives in Port." Journal and Guide January 31, 1925, p. 1.

When Booker T. Washington arrived in Richmond from Philadelphia, Garvey and many of his followers were there to meet the ship which was bound for Havana.

372. "Black Cross Ship Put In Home Port After Ill-Fated Trip." Journal and Guide, June 6, 1925, p. 2.

After much trouble at sea, the Booker T. Washington returned to port. The ship has set sail for South America and the West Indies.

373. "Black Line Promoters Indicted." New York Times, February 17, 1922, p. 26.

Garvey and three of his associates were charged with using the mail to defraud Blacks into investing in the Black Star Line.

374. "Black Magic Fails Again." Independent, Vol. 120, June 23, 1928, p. 586.

Articles give a very brief sketch of Garvey's Movement and some discussion to a meeting organized by Garvey that was scheduled to take place in London in 1928.

375. "Black Moses Off for Federal Pen Cell Here Today." Atlanta Constitution, February 7, 1925, p. 10.

Arrested in Harlem, Garvey was to have been sent to Atlanta after he failed to appear in federal court on his appeal for mail fraud had been denied.

376. "Black Nationalism: The Early Debate." Studies On The Left, Vol. 4, Summer, 1964, pp. 50 - 58.

The three documents in this study are concerned with the development of Black Nationalism in 1919 and 1920 and centers around the Movement and personality of Garvey. Interviewed were Marcus Garvey, founder of the UNIA, W. E. B. DuBois, a Founder of the NAACP, and Editor of The Crisis, and Chandler Owen, Co-Editor of The Messenger. The editor felt that although the interviewer was hostile to all three men, the interview was as accurate as his understanding would allow. The interviews were made for the private use of the National Civic Federation.

377. "Black Star Line Has $31.12 In Banks, Says Accountant." New York Amsterdam News, June 6, 1923, pp. 1, 6.

An accountant testified that stock bonds were missing and over $750.000 worth of shares were sold with only $31.12 accountable.

378. "Blaming It On Garvey." Crusader, Vol. 4, February, 1921, p. 9.

The writer takes exception to a letter by Mr. Herbert of the Urban League to the New York Globe. It said that the reason Whites are not hiring Blacks is that they have no need for their services nor do they desire to help them. If they are telling Blacks to go to Garvey for jobs, it is their way of weakening the morale of Blacks and to create racial problems by holding one group responsible for the ills of the entire country.

379. "By Garvey Mass Meeting Held." Journal and Guide, May 9, 1925.

The local UNIA celebrated Garvey Day on May 3. Various speakers outlined the alleged injustices done to Garvey and a telegram sent to President Coolidge urging the release of Garvey.

380. "Calls Garvey Good Orator, Poor Businessman, and Robber." New York Amsterdam News, May 30, 1923, pp. 1, 6.

Captain Adrian Richardson testified about the Black Star Line. Leo Healy who sold a ship to Garvey also testified. They said he was a good orator but a poor businessman.

381. Calvin, Floyd J. "The NAACP vs. the UNIA." New York Amsterdam News, February 21, 1923, p. 12.

The author looks at the work of the NAACP and that of the UNIA. Calvin felt that both groups denote progress. One wishes to advance and one wishes to progress. One's objective is to build the historic Motherland of Africa and the other fights for equality in America. The programs of the UNIA are business, self-respect, racial pride, racial consciousness, and general uplifting. The NAACP Program is civil rights. The author concludes that what needs to be done is to advance and progress and forget leadership differences.

382. "Constitutional Rights." Time, Vol. 1, June 18, 1923, p. 5.

Marcus Garvey continued to conduct his own defense in his trial on mail fraud. Many witnesses took the stand for Garvey. Some testified regarding his West Indian trip on the Black Star Line Ship. On at least three occasions, the ship almost sank.

383. "Conviction of Garvey Resented By Negroes." Atlanta Constitution, July 17, 1923, p. 5.

The Associated Press in Washington, DC received many letters and telegrams from Blacks throughout the country protesting the conviction of Marcus Garvey.

384. "Court Room Is Jammed As The Trial Goes On." Journal and Guide, June 3, 1923, pp. 1, 5.

As the Garvey trial continued, one of the most damaging witnesses was Harry Watkis, who was a stock salesman for the Black Star Line. He told of a 40 day trip Garvey and his officers took, including a band, to sell stock.

385. "Cox Again Praises Garvey: Mistaken About Prosecution." Journal and Guide, August 15, 1925, p. 1.

Speaking at a UNIA meeting, Major Earnest Cox said he failed to see why intelligent Blacks did not back Garvey's Back to Africa Plan, and he felt that rival organizations were not the cause of Garvey's conviction, but the New York prosecutors were.

386. "Crowd Bids Garvey Goodby." Journal and Guide, December 14, 1927, p. 1.

Almost 1,000 stood in the rain to hear Garvey as he prepared to leave for Jamaica. He said that he would carry on the work for Negro liberation.

387. Crump, Robert A. "Major Cox Denied Right to Speak In Richmond Church." Journal and Guide, September 19, 1925, pp. 1, 5.

The pastor of Sharon Baptist Church said that members of the Anglo-Saxon Club could not speak at the church which was having a UNIA meeting.

388. Cruse, Harold. "The Roots of Black Nationalism." Liberator, Vol. 4, March, 1964, pp. 4 - 6.

This article discusses the earlier Black Movements in comparison with the movement of the 1960s. Discussion is given to the ideals and influences of Garvey and DuBois.

389. "Death Of Marcus Garvey Denied By His Secretary." New York Age, May 25, 1949, p. 1.

Officials of the UNIA denied that Garvey had died in London. They said the newspapers printing the story did not get verification from the UNIA.

390. "Denies That Local UNIA Opposes Garvey Rule." Amsterdam News, September 23, 1925, p. 1.

It was reported that the rumors of the UNIA members were turning against Garvey were false and these rumors were being circulated by one man: James A. Brown, who issued a statement on some of the ills of the organization.

391. "Denounced Garvey In Meeting, Killed While Leaving Church." New York Age, January 13, 1923, p. 1.

Rev. J. W. H. Eason was killed after leaving a meeting in which he had denounced The Marcus Garvey Movement.

392. "Denouncing Race Leaders And Crowning Garvey Was Theme Of UNIA Parade." New York Age, August 9, 1924, pp. 1, 2.

In the first UNIA Parade and Convention since 1922, Garvey denounced several race leaders as traitors and the Black press as corrupt. Praise was given to the later Booker T. Washington; Bishop McGuire, a former enemy, was now considered to be the mouthpiece of the UNIA.

393. "Does Not Want Garvey Deported." Journal and Guide, August 15, 1925, p. 1.

The Richmond Times Dispatch said in an editorial that to deport Garvey would be a mistake and that White America should demand further review of the charges against Garvey. The paper had been impressed with Garvey's plan to return Blacks to Africa.

394. "Dr. DuBois Replies To Bishop C. S. Smith." New York Age, June 25, 1921, p. 5.

Dr. DuBois said Bishop Smith was confusing the Pan-African Congress with the Garvey Movement. He noted that Garvey was not a participant in the Pan-African Congress.

395. "Dr. Eason: Former Garveyite Makes Exposures of UNIA." New York Age, October 14, 1922, p. 7.

Rev. J. W. H. Eason said he was expelled from the Garvey Movement because he asked questions about how finances were being used.

396. "Dr. Lionel Frances Tells Why He Quit As President Of The Philadelphia Division of the UNIA." New York Age, August 30, 1924, pp. 1, 3.

The President of the Philadelphia Branch of the UNIA

"Dr. Lionel Frances Tells Why He Quit As President Of The Philadelphia Division of UNIA."

resigned after announding that Garvey had tried to defraud his branch which had assisted in his release from prison. The organization had lent Garvey money which he refused to repay. The full text of Frances' letter is included.

397. "Elaborate Memorial Service Is Held For Marcus Garvey." New York Age, July 27, 1940, p. 1.

A large memorial service was held for Garvey with Ethel M. Collins and Thomas N. Harvey in charge. A parade from Garvey headquarters to St. Mark's Methodist Church was held before the service.

398. "Emmett Scott Denies That He Knelt Before Garvey." New York Age, August 26, 1922, p. 1.

Emmett Scott wrote The Age to say that he was not present at the "Court Ceremonies" held by Garvey and felt that he was misrepresented. The editor cites the list of people receiving honor which was published by The Negro World. This is the official organ of the UNIA. Mr. Scott's name is included in the listing.

399. "Ex-Leader of Garvey's African Legion Charges Chief With Double-Cross." New York Age, August 9, 1924, p. 2.

After Captain E. L. Gaines refused to allow Garvey to hold his salary for another five years, he resigned his post and Garvey declared his office vacant. Gaines had not been paid any salary during the four years he worked for Garvey and denounced Garvey as a double-crosser and said that no African country would accept Garveyites.

400. "Federal Grand Jury Indicts Marcus Garvey Of The UNIA." New York Age, February 11, 1922, p. 1.

Marcus Garvey was arrested January 12 and was convicted of mail fraud.

401. "Federal Probe of Garvey-Klan Is Not Likely." Journal and Guide, February 10, 1923, p. 1.

An investigation of Garvey's connection with the Klan was not likely. The Justice Department said there were no grounds for an investigation.

402. "Few Hear Garvey At Carnegie." New York Amsterdam News, February 28, 1923, pp. 1, 2.

Garvey spoke at Carnegie Hall on "The Future of the

"Few Hear Garvey At Carnegie."

Black and White Races." Between 1,200 and 1,500 heard him attack the works of W. E. B. DuBois and James Weldon Johnson.

403. $500 Challenge To Black Star Propagandists By Bishop Smith." New York Age, April 16, 1921, p. 1.

AME Bishop C. S. Smith takes issue with the statement that 15 pioneer surveyors and builders had already sailed for Africa on the Black Star Line. His letter challenged this propaganda.

404. "Former Garveyite Writes On Salaries." New York Age, September 23, 1922, pp. 1, 5.

A former member of the UNIA said that the paper had underestimated the salaries of the UNIA officers.

405. "Further Light Is Thrown On Desertion Of Garvey By Influential Leaders." New York Age, September 6, 1924, p. 10.

Several leaders of the UNIA had resigned their posts and most stated that Garvey had a disregard for their personal rights, treated them with contempt, and often did not pay their salaries. Some of the leaders who resigned were Gabriel Johnson, E. L. Gaines, and Dr. Lionel Francis.

406. "Garvey." New York Age, June 30, 1923, p. 4.

During his trial Garvey had the opportunity to show his greatest strength, but instead showed his greatest weakness by his blasphemous attitude in court, concludes the editor.

407. "Garvey." Crisis, Vol. 29, December, 1924, p. 86.

The editor notes Robert Minor's article on "Head Handkerchief Negro Leaders" in the October issue of the Liberator. He felt that Garvey did everything to make himself the "white man's nigger" in the eyes of the White ruling class and, at the same time, a "Negro Moses" in the eyes of suffering Blacks. Also cites his friendship with the Ku Klux Klan.

408. "Garvey About Gone." Messenger, June, 1923, Vol. 5, p. 748.

In a series of mass meetings exposing the fallacy of Garvey's Program, The Messenger launched the "Garvey Must Go!" Campaign. Case after case against Garvey has been filed against him and he is losing his appeal to the people, concludes the editor.

409. "Garvey Adherents In Street Parade." New York Amsterdam News, August 5, 1925, p. 3.

In the annual parade and celebration of the UNIA, banners were carried stating that although Garvey was in prison, Garveyism lives on. It was literally Marcus Garvey Day in Harlem.

410. "Garvey Alliance Denied By Cox." Journal and Guide, August 1, 1925, p. 3.

Major Earnest Cox sent a letter to the paper saying that he was not a member of the UNIA, but that he and Garvey believed in the same ideas. His book, Let My People Go, was dedicated to Garvey.

411. "Garvey and Moton." New York Age, October 28, 1922, p. 4.

Garvey spoke out against Dr. Robert R. Moton who was touring the country speaking on Africans' needs. Since he was not a member of Garvey's Movement, Garvey felt he was invading his territory.

412. "Garvey Appeal Argued." New York Amsterdam News, January 21, 1925, p. 1.

Garvey's mail fraud appeal was argued in the US Circuit Court. His sentence was to be five years in prison and a $1,000 fine.

413. "Garvey's Appeal For Bail Denied By Judge Rogers, Circuit Court." New York Age, June 20, 1923, p. 1.

Garvey was denied bail pending appeal of his conviction on mail fraud.

414. "Garvey As An Imitator." New York Age, July 5, 1924, p. 4.

This editorial expressed surprise at Garvey for using the same publicity methods as the NAACP in advertising the UNIA. This new scheme, "The Colonization of Africa By Negroes As Solution Of Race Problem, which was supposed to develop Liberia as a future home for Blacks.

415. "Garvey Backs Down In Fight With Defender." Chicago Defender, August 5, 1921.

A suit brought against The Chicago Defender by Garvey was thrown out when Garvey failed to file for a continuance. The Defender had won $5,000 in a libel suit against Garvey.

416. "Garvey Believes Conviction Just." Messenger, August, 1923, Vol. 5, p. 781.

Garvey was given a five year sentence for mail fraud and since he had not gone on the hunger strike which he said he would do if he felt the verdict was unjust, The Messenger, concluded that he felt the verdict was just. He made an appeal for a new trial.

417. "Garvey Convicted: Locked Up Without Bail." New York Amsterdam News, June 20, 1923, pp. 1, 6.

Garvey was convicted on the strength of a single letter. A railroad porter had purchased five shares of stock in the Black Star Line through the mail.

418. "Garvey Defended By Major Cox As 'A Great Leader.'" Journal and Guide, August 8, 1925, pp. 1, 6.

The paper questioned Major Cox about Garvey. He admitted that the Black Star Line's failure was a financial loss and blamed Garvey's downfall on rivals, Jews, and Catholics.

419. "Garvey Defense Drags Along As Lawyers Tilt." Journal and Guide, June 16, 1923, p. 1.

Judge Mack warned Garvey that the defense proceedings must be speeded up. Many of Garvey's witnesses matched him in a battle of words.

420. "Garvey Denounced by Government of Liberia." Chicago Defender, July 16, 1921, p. 1.

Bishop C. S. Smith of Detroit received a letter from Edwin Barclay, Secretary of State of Liberia stating that the Liberian government did not endorse Garvey's contemplated political manifestation in Africa. The Liberian bonds Garvey had attempted to float were also denounced.

421. "Garvey Dies In England." New York Age, June 15, 1940, p. 1.

Marcus Garvey died in London one month after his death was falsely reported. He had suffered a stroke in January, 1940.

422. "Garvey Discharges Lawyer, Pleads Own Case." Journal and Guide, May 26, 1923, p. 1.

After nearly a year's delay, Garvey's trial for mail fraud began. The case was outlined and a list of some of the witnesses are included.

423. "Garvey Disclaims Editorial on Cox and John Powell." Journal and Guide, August 29, 1925, pp. 1, 3.

Garvey sent a letter to his paper, The Negro World, asking his disapproval of an editorial against the Anglo-Saxon Club. Garvey regarded the editorial as an insult upon his two friends, Major Cox and John Powell.

424. "Garvey Dodges Libel Suit, But Loses in End." Chicago Defender, May 21, 1921, p. 1.

Marcus Garvey had to pay $5,000 to the Chicago Defender for libelous statements made in his paper against the editor of the Defender.

425. "Garvey Envoy Suing For $8,500 Bail Pay." New York Age, January 6, 1923, p. 1.

John Sydney de Bourg was envoy of the UNIA to the Western Province of the West Indies; he said he was not paid his salary from 1920 - 1922.

426. "Garvey Exposed and Denounced Charges to US Attorney." Journal and Guide, February 3, 1923, pp. 1, 4,

Eight prominent Black citizens sent a letter to US Attorney General Harry M. Daugherty charging Garvey and the UNIA with intimidation and murder. His organization spreads distrust and hatred of Whites, was in search of easy money, class riots, murdered J. W. H. Eason, and victimized the ignorant, said the editor.

427. "Garvey Followers Asked to Finance Leader's Vacation." New York Age, October 6, 1023, p. 8.

Garvey denounced George W. Harris, ex-alderman ot the Twenty-First District. Also, envelopes were passed out for contributions for Garvey's vacation.

428. "Garvey Given Maximum Sentence of Five Years in Prison, Fined $1,000." New York Age, June 30, 1923, p. 1.

The financial affairs of the UNIA officers caused the judge to give Garvey the maximum sentence. In addition to the $1,000 fine, he had to pay the court costs.

429. "Garvey, Great Prophet, Says Bishop Ransom." Journal and Guide, December 17, 1927, p. 1.

Bishop Reverdy Ransom said that the principles of the UNIA leader would never die. Like all prophets, Garvey had been stoned, imprisoned, and banished.

430. "Garvey Holds Court." New York Age, August 19, 1922, p. 1.

At the Third Annual Convention of the UNIA, Garvey bestowed distinguished titles on many known and unknown people.

431. "Garvey Is Calling Witnesses For The Defense This Week." New York Age, June 9, 1923, p. 1.

The prosecution concluded its case against Garvey's accountants investigating the books of the Black Star Line found only $31.75 in assets with $731,432 missing. Garvey was acting as his own counsel.

432. "Garvey Is Convicted." Journal and Guide, June 23, 1923, p. 1.

Marcus Garvey was convicted and faced a large fine and long imprisonment. The prosecution called him treacherous, unscrupulous, and shrewd. Upon leaving on his conviction, Garvey violently accused the prosecution and jury of an attempt to make him relent.

433. "Garvey Is Freed: To Be Deported." Atlanta Constitution, November 24, 1927, p. 1.

Garvey was to be deported as an undesirable alien after his prison sentence for mail fraud.

434. "Garvey Liberated: To Be Deported." Atlanta Constitution, November 27, 1927, p. 1.

Marcus Garvey, "The Black Ponzi," was on his way back to Jamaica as an undesirable alien after his prison term on mail fraud was commuted.

435. "Garvey Loses Appeal to US Supreme Court for Review of His Case." New York Age, March 28, 1925, p. 1.

The United States Supreme Court refused to review the case of Marcus Garvey who was serving a prison sentence for mail fraud. No explanation was given for the refusal. Garvey was reported to be working as a dishwasher in the prison kitchen.

436. "Garvey Loses In Wage Suit." New York Age, December 6, 1924, p. 2.

Captain E. L. Gaines won his suit against Garvey. He was granted $7,500 in back pay from the UNIA.

437. "Garvey Men Found Guilty." New York Amsterdam News, March 28, 1923, p. 1.

Two followers of Garvey's, William Shakespere and

"Garvey Men Found Guilty."

and Constantine Dyer, were found guilty of murdering Rev. J. W. H. Eason. Formerly a Garvey supporter, Eason was murdered when he split with Garvey and became the principal witness in the mail fraud case against Garvey. Eason had also charged that Garvey embezzled the UNIA funds.

438. "Garvey Men In New Orleans Charged With Inciting A Riot." New York Age, January 27, 1923, p. 1.

Ten officers of the New Orleans UNIA were arrested and evidence was seized relating to the assassination of Rev. J. W. H. Eason.

439. "Garvey Names Committee of Four to Administer UNIA Affairs Under His Dictation." New York Age, June 30, 1923, p. 1.

During his prison sentence at Leavenworth, Garvey appointed his wife, Secretary R. L. Poston, Leader William A. Sherrell, and Chancellor Clifford Bourne to lead the UNIA under his dictates.

440. "Garvey Parade Brings Harlem to the Streets." New York Age, August 9, 1924, p. 3.

The new doctrine of the UNIA was a Black Christ. A Pageant was held and a canvas symbolizing "The Black Man of Sorrow" was displayed.

441. "Garvey Petitions Four Into Capitol." Journal and Guide, August 4, 1923, p. 1.

Efforts to obtain bail for Garvey had failed, and a petition on his behalf was sent to the White House. His supporters felt that bail had been granted to others for worse offenses and that denial of bail was more dangerous than the crime he had committed.

442. "Garvey Pleads Own Case In Federal Court." New York Amsterdam News, May 23, 1923, pp. 1, 6.

After almost a year of postponements, the mail fraud trial of Garvey began. Assisted by two White attorneys, Garvey pleaded his own case. The prosecution called several witnesses including Edgar Gray, former Secretary to Garvey.

443. "Garvey Puts Blame For His Downfall on Mulatto Negroes." New York Age, June 30, 1923, p. 1.

Garvey felt that most of his problems came for his own race because they resented Black leadership.

444. "Garvey Released From Tombs for $15,000 Cash Bail." New York Age, September 15, 1923, p. 1.

After putting up $15,000 cash, Garvey was released from jail on September 10. An appeal of his conviction was scheduled for October.

445. "Garvey Release Meeting Sunday." Journal and Guide, December 24, 1927, p. 7.

A celebration was held at the local UNIA office celebrating the release of Marcus Garvey.

446. "Garvey Scores." New York Age, August 26, 1922, p. 4.

At the UNIA, the Bible Society offered free bibles to those in attendance. The offer was rejected and it was proposed that the bibles be distributed to sections of the South.

447. "Garvey Self-Convicted." New York Age, June 30, 1923, p. 4.

This editorial expressed that Garvey convicted himself by trying to act as his own counsel. His blind arrogance caused him to fail to get competent people to carry out his ideas resulting in squandering of the funds he had collected, concludes the editor.

448. "Garvey Sentence Upheld." Journal and Guide, February 7, 1925, p. 1.

The United States Circuit Court of Appeals upheld the five year sentence and $1,000 fine delivered by Judge Mack in June, 1923.

449. "Garvey Should Be Deported." New York Age, September 6, 1924, p. 4.

An outsider gives his view of a UNIA meeting he attended in which Garvey spoke of "putting away" his detractors. Garvey even named persons whom he felt should be silenced. There had been many reports of threats to citizens who said or displayed any resentments toward the UNIA. This editorial stated that if Garvey was allowed to continue the UNIA would rival the Ku Klux Klan.

450. "Garvey Starts Defense Fund for Assassins of Eason." Journal and Guide, January 27, 1923, p. 1.

Garvey started a defense fund for two members of the New Orleans UNIA who were accused of murdering J. W. H. Eason. Eason had been a star witness against Garvey in his trial for mail fraud.

451. "Garvey Still Dreams Of An African Empire." Journal and Guide, March 17, 1923, p. 1.

Marcus Garvey spoke at a local UNIA meeting and told his followers to take affirmative action to establish an independent nation in Africa.

452. "Garvey Storm Center in New York Strife." Atlanta Constitution, November 24, 1927, p. 1.

The editor cites Garvey as the Leader of the "Back to Africa" Movement that caused strife among Black circles for many years. Police have often been called to break up fights between his friends and foes.

453. "Garvey Supporter Threatened Witness and is Sent to Jail." New York Age, June 2, 1923, p. 1.

A subway porter and Garvey supporter was jailed when he threatened a witness in the case.

454. "Garvey To Enter Politics." New York Age, September 19, 1923, p. 1.

In his first meeting after his release from prison, Garvey advised his followers to become citizens, register, and be prepared to vote. Blaming his troubles on "jealous Negroes," Garvey said that his own race was mispresenting him. In urging his followers to vote, he said they could demand that the government send them to Africa.

455. "Garvey Treated 'Em Rough." New York Age, November 10, 1922, p. 4.

Talks about Garvey's speech at the North Carolina State Fair in which he said that he got there by means of the White man's railroad cars and was speaking at the White man's fair. He said if he had to depend on Blacks, he would be walking six months to get there.

456. "Garvey Trial Set." Journal and Guide, January 20, 1923, p. 1.

Garvey's trial was set to begin on February 5. He was charged with selling fraudulent stocks through the mails.

457. "Garvey Turns To Song Writing While Prisoner." Journal and Guide, October 1, 1927, p. 1.

Garvey wrote a song, "Keep Cool" in which he talks about having hope and no bitterness for being in prison. The song was to inspire courage, hope, and charity for the oppressed and depressed.

458. "Garvey Unfairly Attacked." Messenger, Vol. 4, April, 1922, p. 387.

This editorial opposed the article in The Chicago Defender in which Roscoe C. Simmons said that if Garvey did not like this country he should go back to Jamaica. He felt that Garvey had done both good and harm but criticism should be on a fair basis and not just based on nationality.

459. "Garvey's Black Religion." New York Age, August 9, 1924, p. 4.

This editorial stated that Garvey suffered from an inferiority complex. His desire to create a Black religion was seen as evidence that he could not deal with anyone or anything of another race. His creation of a Black Christ and a Black Madonna was his way of getting even with the White race.

460. "Garvey's Gone!" Messenger, Vol. 5, April, 1923, p. 759.

The editor notes that Garvey threatened his critics at a conviction in 1922 and by June 1923, was no longer on the scene.

461. "Garvey's Klan Parlay Revealed By Imperial Giant of Ku Klux Klan." New York Amsterdam News, February 14, 1923, p. 7.

Edward Young Clark, Imperial Giant of the Ku Klux Klan, was subpoenaed as a witness in the case against Garvey. Clark testified that Garvey had visited the Klan in Atlanta and had subsequently advised Blacks to stop fighting the Klan and plan to return to Africa instead. Garvey was denounced in the press and Clark testified that the visit spread dissension in the Klan.

462. "Garvey's Liner Held at Panama on Libel Order." Journal and Guide, April 11, 1925, p. 1.

One of Marcus Garvey's ships was seized in Panama after it was libeled for wages by its former master and other officers.

463. "Garvey's New Friends." Journal and Guide, August 15, 1925, p. 12.

This editorial noted that the Richmond Times-Dispatch does not want Garvey deported because he was in favor of the migration of Blacks to Africa. It was also noted that Africa was under the rule of European Whites who have warned Garvey to stay out of Africa.

464. "Garvey's Officers Draw More Than $143,000 Yearly." New York Age, August 19, 1922, p. 2.

Previous figures reported in this paper had estimated officials received $50,000 in salaries but it was later learned that it was more like $143,000. A list of the officers and their salaries are given.

465. "Garvey's Paper Repudiates Cox and John Powell." Journal and Guide, August 22, 1925, p. 1.

In the Negro World, it was cited that Garvey and the UNIA were not proponents of the same ideas as the Anglo-Saxon Clubs, an organization dedicated to saving the White race. The paper stated that they had no right to use the Garvey Movement to further their propaganda plans.

466. "Garvey's Social Equality Cables." Messenger, Vol. 3, October, 1921, p. 259.

Garvey had begun to preach of Black inferiority to the Black and White races. His rage was directed against W. E. B. DuBois. He also said that if Blacks admit they are social inferiors, they admit they are entitled to inferior treatment.

467. "Garvey's SS Washington On Way to West Indies." New York Amsterdam News, January 21, 1925, p. 9.

Thousands of UNIA members were at Pier 75 to see the SS Booker T. Washington sail. They paid $1.00 admission fee. Garvey explained that it was necessary to get White officers because there were few competent Blacks and because of the treachery of his first Black Seaman.

468. "Garvey's Successor Pleads for Unity of Negro Organiations." New York Age, February 22, 1941, p. 3.

At a mass meeting of the Negro People of The World, President General Stewart of the UNIA, argued that Blacks should stop fighting against each other and fight for an ideal.

469. "Garvey's Trial Is Proceeding Slowly Towards Its Closing." New York Age, June 16, 1923, p. 1.

In the final sessions of the trial, Garvey accused the Vice President of the Black Star Lines as a "jinx" and had seen other companies bankrupt.

470. "Garveyites Appeal To President Coolidge." Journal and Guide, August 25, 1923, p. 1.

Garvey supporters asked President Coolidge to look

"Garveyites Appeal to President Coolidge."

into the actions of Prosecuting Attorney Maxwell Mattuck and Department of Justice Agent, E. Amos, during the trial of Marcus Garvey.

471. "Garveyites Draft Petition to President Harding in Behalf of Their Imprisoned Leader." New York Age, July 7, 1923, p. 1.

Fifteen hundred UNIA members held a mass meeting and asked for an investigation of the conduct at the trial and conviction of their leader.

472. "Garveyites Get Year for Disturbance at Anti-Garvey Meeting." New York Age, January 27, 1923, p. 1.

A man was charged with shooting at a policeman during an anti-Garvey meeting. He received a fine and a one year sentence.

473. "German Appeal to Garvey." Nation, Vol. 113, December 28, 1921, p. 769.

Reprint of an open letter to Garvey which first appeared in the Munchner Neueste Nachtichten (Munich) November 25, 1921. Letter was from the German Emergency League against the Black Horror. The letter discusses opposition to the use of Black soldiers by France, and congratulates Garvey for his protesting to the Washington Conference that Africans had not been consulted in the composition of the Treaty of Versailles or in the partition of Africa.

474. "High Official of UNIA Potentate Gabriel Johnson Disgusted, Has Quit Office." New York Age, August 23, 1924, p. 2.

The former Mayor of Monrovia, Liberia and the next highest officer in the UNIA resigned his post in February but Garvey kept it a secret fearing loss of financial support. Johnson had to find extra work because his salary from Garvey was insufficient. A copy of Johnson's letter is included.

474. "Hundreds Hear Marcus Garvey." Journal and Guide, November 10, 1923, p. 1.

Speaking at a local UNIA meeting, Garvey vowed to continue the fight for African Redemption. He criticized his opponents and said that jail held no terror for him.

475. "James Stewart Named Acting President-General At UNIA Meeting." New York Age, August 31, 1940, p. 1.

James Stewart of Cleveland was named acting President-

"James Stewart Named Acting President-General at UNIA Meeting."

General of the UNIA. Installation was to be on September 22. Delegate pledged to forward the cause of Garveyism and the UNIA.

476. "Judgment Against UNIA." Amersterdam News, October 17, 1923, p. 7.

"Sir" Sydney de Bourg was awarded $9,781 in back pay from the UNIA. He was one of the principal witnesses against Garvey during his trial.

477. "Liberia and Garvey." New York Age, July 26, 1924, p. 4.

This editorial notes that the Liberian government was well aware of the dangers of the Garvey Movement when it issued a statement that Garveyites would not be allowed in Liberia. It was said that Garvey had a valuable gift of making converts to his ideas but lacked the character and capacity to use his power to achieve useful ends.

478. "Liberia Bars All Garveyites." New York Age, July 19, 1924, p. 1.

Dr. Ernest Lyon, Liberian Counsel-General in the United States, issued a warning that Garveyites were not welcome in Liberia. The official announcement was given.

479. "Liberian Government Disapproves of Garvey." New York Age, July 16, 1921, p. 1.

Bishop C. S. Smith received a letter from Edwin Barclay, Secretary of State of Liberia, in which he stated that Garvey's Movement was not endorsed by the Liberian government. A copy of the letter is included.

480. "Liberia Objects to Garvey Policy." Atlanta Constitution, August 27, 1924, p. 2.

Ernest Lyon, Consul General for Liberia, advised the Washington government that Liberia was opposed in principal and in fact to the policies of Garvey and the UNIA.

481. "Major Cox Defends Marcus Garvey's Migration Scheme." Journal and Guide, July 4, 1925, p. 1.

Major E. S. Cox, author of White America and Let My People Go, was in agreement with Garvey's program of Black Migration to Africa. He felt that the government should finance these trips.

482. Malliet, A. M. Wendell. "If Garvey Were In Harlem Today, Would (Father) Divine Vanish?" New York Amsterdam News, June 12, 1937, p. 13.

The writer argues that Garvey's hold and spectacular leadership would have created a situation in Harlem and Negro America like that which has developed in Germany under Adolph Hitler. Garveyism would have emboldened the mob and engendered intraracial and interracial strife. He concludes that Garvey's personal leadership would have encouraged the masses to take things into their own hands whenever a situation was sufficiently provoking - if Garvey were in Harlem today (1937).

483. "Marcus Garvey and Party Visit Tuskegee Institute." New York Age, November 24, 1923, p. 5.

Garvey and his party stopped at Tuskegee Institute for two days. He spoke and gave $50 to the school.

484. "Marcus Garvey and the NAACP." Crisis, February, 1928, p. 51.

This article focuses on conflicts between Garvey and the NAACP. However, the intent appears to be to show that the NAACP was not an enemy of Garvey's. The article cites other articles published in the Crisis concerning Garvey.

485. "Marcus Garvey Convicted and Held in Tombs Until Thursday For His Sentence." New York Age, June 23, 1923, p. 1.

Garvey was found guilty of mail fraud but three fellow officers and codefendants were acquitted. His plea for bail was refused and he was to be jailed until his sentencing.

486. "Marcus Garvey Draws the Color Line." Journal and Guide, July 21, 1923, p. 10.

This artucle compares Garvey and Booker T. Washington stating that Washington was just as dictatorial and self-centered as Garvey, but he had capable and honest people working with him. The author concludes that Garvey brought his troubles on himself and was incapable of handling the men and money in his organization.

487. "Marcus Garvey's End." Journal and Guide, July 7, 1923, p. 10.

This editorial from the Baltimore Afro-American notes that the tragedy in the Garvey case was that the faith of a struggling race was once again shaken by this fiasco of Black leadership.

488. "Marcus Garvey Hires George Gordon Battle to Argue His Appeal." New York Age, December 20, 1924, p. 9.

It was estimated that Garvey paid his counsel $8,000 to represent him in his appeal for conviction of mail fraud. Four printed briefs containing 2,800 pages of testimony were presented.

489. "Marcus Garvey's Idea Will Not Be Deported." Journal and Guide, December 10, 1927, p. 16.

In Mary Church Terrell's column, she stated that even though Garvey had been deported, his ideas will live on even after he is dead.

490. "Marcus Garvey In Court As Plaintiff in Forgery Charge." New York Age, November 15, 1924, p. 1.

Garvey charged Harry E. Arnold, a former employee with misuse of funds for the Black Cross Navigation and Trading Company. It was cited that Arnold stole UNIA certificates, buttons, and literature and tried to sell them illegally.

491. "Marcus Garvey Is Indicted On False Income Tax Returns." New York Age, August 9, 1924, p. 1.

Garvey was indicted on three counts of income tax evasion for the year 1921. He pleaded not guilty and was released on $2,500 bail. Returning to the UNIA Convention, Garvey said he felt his arrest and previous conviction of mail fraud was part of a political attack against him.

492. "Marcus Garvey Is Now Admitted To Bail." Journal and Guide, September 8, 1923, p. 1.

Garvey's bail was set at $25,000 upon the recommendation of US District Attorney William Hayward.

493. "Marcus Garvey." Messenger, Vol. 4, August, 1922, p. 471.

Reprint of an editorial in Ryan's Weekly (Tacoma, Washington) discussing Garvey's speech at Valhalia Hall in which he talked about redeeming Africa and made an appeal for members in the UNIA. His abstract and vague statements only confused his listeners. This editorial stated that Garvey should be left "severely alone."

494. "Marcus Garvey Must Go!" Messenger, Vol. 4, October, 1922, p. 508.

The Campaign, "Marcus Garvey Must Go!" was inaugurated by the Friends of Negro Freedom. In August, a rally

"Marcus Garvey Must Go!"

was held in New York to address itself to Garvey's claims. Some of the speakers were William Pickens, A. Philip Randolph, Chandler Owens, and Robert A. Bagnall. They felt that Garvey had entered into a deal with the Ku Klux Klan, his African Policy was unsound, his personality was paranoid, and he should be deported.

495. "Marcus Garvey Names Three To Carry On Work." New York Age, February 14, 1925, p. 2.

Before he departed for prison in Atlanta, Garvey named his successors. They were William Lee Van Sherrill, Clifford S. Bourne, and G. E. Carter. He urged his followers to support these officers. He also urged them to cheer up for their enemies would pay for their sins.

496. "Marcus Garvey." New York Age, May 25, 1940, p. 12.

This article cites Garvey's death as being erroneously reported in London. The author concludes that although he failed in his efforts, he tried to do something for his race and was willing to sacrifice all for the cause of race advancement.

497. "Marcus Garvey." New York Amsterdam News, June 27, 1923, p. 12.

It was proven that Garvey had squandered money, some of which was gotten through illegal use of the mails. It was hoped that the UNIA would see Garvey as he really was, concludes the author.

498. "Marcus Garvey Out." Amsterdam News, November 30, 1927, p. 20.

This editorial looks at the magical influence Garvey had on the Black Race. Even though Blacks lost money to Garvey, few regreted the loss. Garvey made Blacks feel that his cause was theirs and that no one was too humble to work for Black redemption.

499. "Marcus Garvey Plans World Tour To Last More Than Year." New York Age, January 13, 1923, p. 1.

Garvey was to tour the world to Speak to American Whites and European working class.

500. "Marcus Garvey Release Week." Journal and Guide, June 11, 1927, p. 12.

June 12 - 19 was designated as Marcus Garvey Release Week by the UNIA. Although the editor of this news-

"Marcus Garvey Release Week."

paper did not agree with the principles of the Garvey Movement, he was in favor of a pardon for Garvey.

501. "Marcus Garvey Should Be Pardoned." Journal and Guide, June 4, 1927, p. 14.

It was reported that Garvey's health was failing after two years in prison. It was felt that Garvey had been justly punished and that he should be pardoned.

502. "Marcus Garvey Still At It." New York Age, November 10, 1923, p. 4.

Marcus Garvey was still preaching his "Back to Africa" propaganda. This editorial stated that he only was playing into the hands of the enemy by preaching Ku Klux Klan sentiments.

503. "Marcus Garvey! The Black Imperial Wizard Becomes Messenger Boy of The White Ku Klux Kleagle." Messenger, Vol. 4, July, 1922, p. 437.

In a New Orleans speech, Garvey said that he could not blame the White man for Jim Crowing him because he was Black. This editorial denounced Garvey as a West Indian demagogue who preyed upon ignorant men and women who thought he was some sort of Moses. It urged all ministers, editors, and others interested in the race, to drive Garveyism out of this country.

504. "Marcus Garvey: The Man, An Intimate Study of A Leader's Personality." New York Age, October 21, 1922, p. 1.

Talks about how Marcus Garvey started the UNIA, his values, and his publications.

505. "Menace of Garveyism." New York Age, August 16, 1924, p. 4.

This editorial denounced the statement made at the UNIA Convention that it was unsafe for anyone to walk the streets of Harlem without a Garvey button. Garvey and his associates vent their hostilities against those of their own race who fail to pay tribute to him and financially support his schemes. The editorial said that Garvey should be deported.

506. Miller, Kelly. "Why Garvey Should Be Pardoned." Journal and Guide, August 27, 1927, p. 1.

The author felt that Garvey should be pardoned. He argues that the law had been vindicated and no further

Miller, Kelly.

purpose could be served by further imprisonment of Garvey.

507. "Mr. Garvey's Praise of Dr. Washington and His Work." Journal and Guide, November 24, 1923, p. 11.

Marcus Garvey paid tribute to Booker T. Washington after visiting Tuskegee Institute. He said he saw men working with their hands in dignified labor, thus preparing them to become better African citizens.

508. "Negro Delegates March." New York Times, August 2, 1922, p. 17.

The Third Annual Convention of the UNIA was held with Marcus Garvey presiding in his red and green velvet robe. Eight thousand delegates marched in the afternoon parade.

509. "Negroes Cheer As Garvey Sails, Jamaica Bound." Atlanta Constitution, December 3, 1927, p. 9.

After serving more than two years in an Atlanta prison, Garvey sailed for Jamaica. Five hundred Blacks stood on the shore and shouted "God Save Our President!"

510. "Negro Prosperity Overrated." Crusader, Vol. 4, February, 1921, p. 27.

In this letter, James Herbert of the Urban League, said that White employees have a false notion of Black prosperity and noted they tell Blacks looking for work to go to their race for jobs. "Go to Marcus Garvey - he had factories and ships," is what Whites are telling Black workers. Mr. Herbert felt there were not enough jobs in the Black community to meet demands.

511. "Nigerian Progress Union." The Spokesman, Vol. 1, February, 1925, p. 16.

Organized by Mrs. Marcus Garvey (Amy Ashwood), the Nigerian Progress Union was to educate the masses of Southern Nigerians to help solve the social and economic problems of Nigeria, to promote racial pride among them, to foster the spirit of independence, and to support the education of African girls in England.

512. "No Bail For Garvey." New York Amsterdam News, June 27, 1923, pp. 1, 3.

It was argued that Garvey's offense was not extraditable and he would flee if released on bail. Federal Judge Henry Rogers refused bail for him but Garvey

"No Bail For Garvey."

said prison would not deter him from his task - the freedom of Africa.

513. "Obituary of Marcus Garvey in the New York Times." New York Times, June 11, 1940.

The newspaper printed, in part, " . . . He no more represented the Negro in this country than Mr. Capone or Mr. Hampmann the White race.

514. Peet, H. H. "Interview With Marcus Garvey." Southern Workman, Vol. 57, October, 1928, p. 423.

An interview conducted after Garvey's imprisonment in the US and his subsequent deportation to the West Indies. This interview does not focus on the events surrounding his imprisonment but instead focuses on Garvey's continued commitment to the betterment of the Black Race.

515. "Pickens Pleads For Release of Marcus Garvey." Journal and Guide, August 6, 1927, p. 1.

William Pickens of the NAACP came out in favor of releasing Garvey on the grounds of "social justice."

516. "President General of UNIA, James R. Stewart, Speaks Here." New York Age, May 17, 1941, p. 3.

President General Stewart of the UNIA spoke to the New York division of the organization on May 11.

517. "Reconsiders Garvey Plea for Pardon." Journal and Guide, November 26, 1927, p. 1.

It was recommended by the special assistant to the Attorney General that the Justice Department reconsider Garvey's plea for a pardon.

518. "S. Agents Raid Garvey Organization In New Orleans." New York Amsterdam News, January 24, 1923, p. 2.

Twenty-one officers and members of the New Orleans UNIA Chapter were arrested during a mass meeting. A raid was made stemming from an investigation into the assassination of J. W. H. Eason, a government witness against Garvey. Evidence was found indicating that Eason's death was planned. Books, letters, and other UNIA documents were seized.

519. "Speakers Declare Garvey Is Victim of Persecutors." Journal and Guide, Marcy 7, 1925, p. 3.

Over 200 people were at Calvary Baptist Church to hear various speakers declare that Garvey was a victim of

"Speakers Declare Garvey Is Victim Of Persecutors."

persecution and a frame-up. They passed a resolution to send to President Coolidge requesting that Garvey be given special consideration.

520. "Suits Follow Suit Against UNIA." New York Amsterdam News, February 4, 1925, p. 7.

Former Garvey Commissioner to the West Indies, James O'Meally sued the UNIA for $7,657 in back pay. Randolph Smith, former Assistant President-General, was suing for $10,000 salary.

521. "The Apothesis of the Ridiculous." New York Age, August 19, 1922, p. 4.

This article reported on the "court ceremonies" at Liberty Hall given by Garvey in which he bestowed dukedoms and knighthoods on serveral people to remind Blacks of the past glories of Ethiopia and the future possibilities of Africa. This editorial felt that the ceremony was ridiculous.

522. "The Lesson of Garvey." New York Age, February 14, 1925, p. 4.

This editorial notes that the lesson to be drawn from Garvey's conviction was the success in business cannot be achieved by empty bluster, and bluff. The methods he used to attract attention and to dupe people aroused interracial prejudice and made him a dangerous element in the community, concluded the author.

523. "The New Garvey Ship Is Now Held At Balboa On Wage Libel By Officers." New York Age, April 4, 1925, p. 1.

Garvey's ship, the "Goethals" was seized after it was libeled for wages for its former master and other officers. The vessel was empty of cargo but had coal and passengers aboard when seized.

524. "The Passing of Garvey." New York Amsterdam News, April 4, 1923, p. 12.

This editorial notes that Garvey is on the way out and must make room for another and that he had lost a great opportunity to serve the Black Races of the World.

525. "The Passing of Garvey." Opportunity, March, 1925, p. 66.

The author noted that Garvey had been sentenced to prison; it wondered about the masses who believed in him and what would happen to their dream.

526. "The Press and 'Back to Africa'." Crisis, October 24, 1922, pp. 273 - 274.

Cites some of the comments of the press on Garvey's Back to Africa Movement. Quotes from The New York Sun, The New York Call, and The New York Telegraph mostly against the movement and Garvey's philosophy.

527. "The Purple Robed Champion of 'African For The Africans'." Literary Digest, September 4, 1920, p. 63.

Marcus Garvey was a combination of dreamer, orator, and shrewd businessman. He proposed the organization of a real modern industrial state in Africa. He did not say how he would obtain Africa from the nation claiming it.

528. "The Spirit of Garveyism." New York Age, May 15, 1926, p. 4.

A delegation met with the US Attorney General to plead for Garvey's release. The delegation claimed that Garvey had been framed by rivals and other jealous leaders. The editorial stated that Garveyism was still running rampant but it could not fool the US authorities into releasing him.

529. Thomas, V. P. "Federal Probe of Murder of Dr. Eason Has Been Ordered." New York Age, January 27, 1923, p. 1.

The UNIA was to be part of the investigation into the assassination of Rev. J. W. H. Eason who had spoken out against the Garvey Movement.

530. Thorpe, Earl E. "Africa In The Thought of Negro Americans." Negro History Bulletin, Vol. 23, No. 1, 1959, pp. 5 - 10.

This article focuses upon the attitudues of various Black leaders toward Africa and Africans. The author examined such prominent Blacks as Phyllis Wheatley, Benjamin Banneker, W. E. B. DuBois, Carter G. Woodson, and Marcus Garvey. The author also discussed the attitudes and views of Black writers, musicians, and artists toward Africa.

531. "To Ask Virginia Congressmen to Aid Garvey." Journal and Guide, November 14, 1925, p. 1.

Local UNIA members signed a petition to send to Washington asking for Garvey's release.

532. "To Deport Garvey." Journal and Guide, August 15, 1925, p. 1.

"To Deport Garvey."

A warrant for Garvey's deportation after he completed his sentence was filed in a hearing before immigration agents.

533. "Trial of Marcus Garvey, Charged With Using Mail to Defraud, In Progress." New York Age, May 26, 1923, p. 1.

The US District Court was beginning its case against Garvey and the UNIA. The charge was using the US mail to defraud through the sale of stock in the Black Line.

534. "Two Thousand Bostonians Want Garvey To Be Released." Journal and Guide, July 2, 1927, p. 1.

The Boston Chapter of the UNIA sponsored a drive for the release of Garvey. A petition with 2,000 signatures was sent to President Coolidge.

535. "UNIA Divisions Plan Convention." Journal and Guide, June 20, 1923, p. 1.

The branches of the UNIA throughout the country were planning a conference to consider their future. They resented Garvey's turning the affairs of the organization over to his wife after his conviction.

536. "UNIA Head On Way Home." Journal and Guide, December, 1927, pp. 1 - 2.

Marcus Garvey was released from prison and sent back to Jamaica. He would not discuss his plans but the UNIA officials noted an appeal to have the deportation lifted.

537. "UNIA Head Urges Support For Dyer Bill." New York Age, January 14, 1922, p. 5.

The UNIA in Connecticut urged citizens to write their congressman in favor of the Dyer Anti-Lynching Bill.

538. "UNIA Local Convention Going On In Berkeley." Journal and Guide, August 13, 1927, p. 3.

Speakers at the local convention pleaded for Garvey's release from prison and advocated his "Nation Building Movement."

539. "UNIA Meeting Successful Event." Journal and Guide, November 12, 1927, p. 2.

The Norfolk branch of the UNIA held a successful meeting where the members were urged to a realization of their civic duties and responsibilities.

540. "UNIA Meeting Draws Crowd." Journal and Guide, November 26, 1927, p. 2.

The Norfolk UNIA Chapter had a successful mass meeting. The guest speaker talked about racial uplift and entertainment was provided.

541. "UNIA Speaker Coming To The City." Journal and Guide, July 2, 1927, p. 4.

The President of the Pittsburgh Branch of the UNIA spoke in Norfolk on July 9 as part of an extensive southern tour.

542. "UNIA Speakers Holding Meeting." Journal and Guide, May 21, 1927, p. 4.

The Acting President of the UNIA, Fred A. Tooter, spoke at the Berkeley Division. Pictures were shown of their progress and a large parade was planned.

543. "What the UNIA (Says It) Has Done." New York Amsterdam News, September 19, 1923, p. 12.

This article from the Negro World cites the things the UNIA has done for Blacks. It gave them incentive to live, killed the inferiority bogey, and removed it from the path of Black progress - the greatest obstacle - false, self-seeking, parasitic leadership.

544. White, Lucien H. "Garvey Resigns But There Is A Long String Attached." New York Age, August 26, 1922, pp. 1, 5.

Marcus Garvey resigned his positions as President General of the UNIA and Provisional President of Africa after it was reported that these positions paid $21,000.

545. "Why Isn't Garvey Tried?" New York Amsterdam News, March 14, 1923, p. 12.

This editorial questioned the reluctance of the Federal Grand Jury to try Garvey. Since his indictment on mail fraud, his trial had been postponed several times. It looked as though the authorities did not have enough evidence to proceed with the case, concludes the author.

546. "Why Not Garvey." Journal and Guide, November 26, 1927, p. 14.

The author lists some people who had been given clemency for worse offenses and wondered why Garvey did not get the same treatment.

547. "Wife of Garvey Goes On Stand In His Defense." New York Amsterdam News, June 13, 1923, pp. 1, 6.

"Wife Of Garvey Goes On Stand In His Defense."

Most of the 48 witnesses testified that Marcus Garvey did not handle money from the sale of stock or sold any stock himself. Mrs. Garvey testified that Garvey never sent circulars through the mail. Garvey used the tactic of serving subpoenae on government agents in order to prove they were hostile witnesses.

7
DISSERTATIONS AND THESES

---

548. Aron, Birgit. "The Garvey Movement." Unpublished Master's Thesis, Columbia University, 1947.

The writer surmises that the Garvey Movement never reached its ultimate goal of African Redemption. The author continues to point out that Garveyism, at least by example, prepared the way for the development of Negro businesses, and created a new attitude on the part of some Negro leaders toward such efforts. Finally, it has contributed to the awakening of a positive racial consciousness among Negroes in America; that is, racial pride rather than a racial inferiority complex. Aron concludes that Garveyism has touched a chord somewhere in the minds of Negroes - the uneducated as well as the most sophisticated of Negroes - and has forced them to face the important though painful and disconcerting question of their future in this country.

549. Avery, Sheldon. "Up From Washington: William Pickens and The Negro Struggle For Equality, 1900 - 1954." Unpublished Doctoral Dissertation, University of Oregon, 1970.

The writer discussed William Pickens' involvement with Marcus Garvey and his Movement. Pickens supported the Movement. While he opposed Garvey's Back to Africa Movement, nevertheless, he was of the opinion that Garvey's Program was the greatest menace of the time to the White world.

550. Burkett, Randall R. "Garveyism As A Religious Movement." Unpublished Doctoral Dissertation, University of Southern California, 1975.

The author examines the religious dimensions of an early Twentieth Century Black Power Movement, the Universal Negro Improvement Association (UNIA). This study discusses the rituals and symbols, the belief system, and the ecclesiological structure of the UNIA. The receptivity of Garvey's "Black Civil Religion" by the clergy is examined to illustrate the range and depth of support among this most influential segment of Black leadership. Dr. Burkett concludes that a case is made for viewing Marcus Garvey as the preeminent Black theologian of the early Twentieth Century, and it is argued that the rituals, beliefs, and institutional framework he articulated taken together constitute the UNIA as a religious movement which can best be described as a form of Black Civil Religion.

551. Goldman, Morris. "The Garvey Movement: 1916 - 1927." Unpublished Master's Thesis, New School for Social Research, 1953.

The writer argues that the Garvey Movement can be regarded as a microcosm of an important aspect of western culture. It transformed racist ideology of the White world which had been developed at the expense of the Black Race in a racist utopia for the benefit of the Black man. The author also points out that the Fascist and semi-Fascist organizations in the United States were working in behalf of Garvey and it is quite conceivable that they contributed for his defense.

552. Jordan, Samuel. "Beyond Contributions: Marcus Garvey As the Object Of A Case Study Approach To Understanding Afro-American Participation In American History and Culture." Unpublished Doctoral Dissertation, Columbia University, 1975.

The main purpose of this study was to provide a theoretical conceptualization of the entire Black group experience in America upon which intelligent curricula decisions, educational policy-making, and, hopefully, practice could be based. This conceptualization can be called the case study approach to understanding Afro-American participation in American history and culture; which, for the purposes of this study, can be defined as an intensive indepth examination in America as reflected in the life of a pivotal Black historical figure around whom these elements coalesced. The research problem then broke down into two parts: (1) identifying the essential elements of the Black American experience, and (2) find a historical figure around whom all of these elements coalesced.

Jordan, John Samuel.

Marcus Garvey and his Back to Africa Movement were found to be ideal as the historical figure; and research revealed, for this writer, five areas of the Black American experience which contain its essential elements: (1) The Fundamental Dialetic, the separate-integrate dilemma which has divided Afro-Americans from the early beginning of their history in this country until the present day; (2)"Double-Consciousness," the disquieting feeling on the part of Black Americans that they are both "Black" and "American" and the effect which this has had upon their attitudes toward America and themselves; (3) Responses to Blackness, the ways Black Americans have responded to their color, their actual and perceived Blackness; (4) Recurring Patterns, the obvious tendency toward repetition found in Afro-American history, and what accounts for this; and (5) Afro-Americans, Africa, and the Pan-African Ideal, the sometimes-negative sometimes-positive attitudes which Afro-Americans have had toward the continent of their origin and their relationships with Africans and the people of African descent throughout the world. Historical analysis was the method used in this examination of Garvey and the Garvey Movement.

553. Lewis, Joan Elaine Wilson. "A Comparative Study of the Marcus Garvey and Black Muslim Movements." Unpublished Master's Thesis, Howard University, 1967.

The title tells what this work is about; she contends that the present day Black Muslim Movement in the United States and the Marcus Garvey Movement are similar in their ideologies and goals. Both Movements have called for total withdrawal of American Blacks from the American society in order to create a social order parallel to the one of their orientation, with their own values, norms, institutions, and customs. The writer gives a historical outline of the growth of the Black Muslim and Marcus Garvey Movements as depicted in prior studies of Black Movements in the United States. She also discusses the historical background of Marcus Garvey and of Elijah Muhammed.

554. Lewis, Rupert. "A Political Study Of Garveyism In Jamaica and London: 1914 - 1940." Unpublished Thesis, University of West Indies, 1971.

The author feels that Garvey's earlier involvement in politics started his relationship with the National Club in Jamaica. He was elected one of the assistant secretaries of the club, which sought to combat privilege and the evils of Colonialism in Jamaica.

555. Palmer, Huber. "Three Black Nationalist Organizations and Their Impact Upon Their Times." Unpublished Doctoral Dissertation, Claremont Graduate School , 1973.

The writer argues that Garveyism had as its impetus a strong program of Black Capitalism coupled with a "Back to Africa" Movement. Garveyism was significant in that it was the first occasion in the history of the Black experience in America that a Mass Movement of such force had been generated solely among Blacks. Furthermore, the respondents to Garveyism were primarily from the lower classes as Garvey himself. The program also had as one of its high priorities the development of a cultural awareness among Blacks. Dr. Palmer concludes that since its inception, Garveyism as a force in the Black community, although waning, never expired. In the East, particularly in the New York area, Garveyism is experiencing a recurrence.

556. Payne, James Chris, II. "A Content Analysis of Speeches and Written Documents of Six Black Spokesmen: Frederick Douglass, W. E. B. DuBois, Martin Luther King Jr., and Malcolm X." Unpublished Doctoral Dissertation, Florida State University, 1970.

This is a computer-assisted, content analysis study which establishes rhetorical norms for the six spokesmen named in the title. Their norms are base-line date which are intended to serve as rhetorical benchmarks to which other spokesmen can be compared. Five texts were selected for each spokesman. The scores for each spokesman's five texts were averaged for each of the the ten scales in order to obtain a mean score for each spokesman on every phycholinguistic scale. Dr. Payne concludes that there is no significant difference between the spokesman's communications directed toward general or audiences which are not predominantly Black.

557. Strickland, Shirley Wilson. "A Functional Analysis of the Garvey Movement." Unpublished Doctoral Dissertation, University of North Carolina at Chapel Hill, 1956.

The writer looked at the Garvey Movement as a sociologically significant phenomenon. She argues that Garvey was an intuitive expert in mass psychology, and a skilled practitioner of the techniques of inciting mass support and enthusiasm. The author concludes that if he had presented a program that was fashioned to contemporary needs, and if he had made his appeal to race-conscious, organized, militant American Negroes, the man with the mission might well have become a prominent leader of the Negro masses in the 1930s.

558. Thompson, Litchfield O'Brien. "Recurring Ideological Themes in the Sociology of Black Nationalists: From the Founding Fathers to Contemporary Analysts." Unpublished Doctoral Dissertation, The University of Oregon, 1975, p. 414.

The author looks at Anglo-Nationalist, Acculturationalist, and Marxist views of Black Nationalists. It demonstrated the relevance of Garveyism and the Black Muslim Movements to Blacks and provides a systematic framework for understanding Black Nationalism. Dr. Thompson concludes that Garveyism, like other Black Nationalistic Movements, is basically though not wholly, a lower class phenomenon, which seeks to address its attention to real social, cultural, political, and economic pressure in Black America. Garveyism is a group ideology which seeks to get beyond this condition by strengthening, perpetuating and/or creating group institutions capable of reducing dependence on White society, concludes the author.

559. Tolbert, Emory Joel. "The Universal Negro Improvement Association In Los Angeles: A Study of Western Garveyism." Unpublished Doctoral Dissertation, University of California, Los Angeles, 1975.

The City of Los Angeles had an active division of the UNIA and was an outgrowth of the Los Angeles Forum, a loosely organized, community based social and benevolent group. The Los Angeles Garveyite leadership were handicapped by their distance from UNIA headquarters in New York City, their desire to encourage local investment by UNIA members against the will of the parent body, and their desire to expand beyond the limited economic and political structure of the New York based UNIA. Dr. Tolbert concludes that the UNIA Chapter in Los Angeles seemed to have been oriented toward religious, family men. In a competitive environment, where Blacks were not central to the economy and relatively few in number, the UNIA performed the function of a Black fraternity.

560. Watkins, Irma. "The DuBois - Garvey Controversy." Unpublished Master's Thesis, Atlanta University, 1971.

The author looks at the Nineteenth Century Pan-African background, DuBois' Pan-African Congress Movement, and the Pan Africanism of Garvey. He discusses Garvey's leadership appeal, his Liberian Project, the controversy between Garvey and DuBois, and the eventual decline of the UNIA. The author felt that despite their personal anagonisms, they were inevitably linked together within the broad context of Pan-Africanism.

561. Weber, Shirley Nash. "The Rhetoric of Marcus Garvey: Leading Spokesman for the Universal Negro Improvement Association In the United States, 1916 - 1929." Unpublished Doctoral Dissertation, University of California, Los Angeles, 1975.

This study describes, analyzes, and critically evaluates the speaking event and the speech of Garvey in an effort to illuminate the basic issues, arguments, and appeals that he used. In examining his strategy, by categorizing them by the agitation strategies of vilification, mythication, legitimation, and objectification, critical evaluations were made as to the potential effect of each in contributing to the success of the rhetoric and the Movement. Dr. Weber concludes that Garvey's rhetoric and the Association overshadowed all current Negro leaders and organizations because of his ability to identify with the masses of Blacks.

562. Zickefoose, Harold Eugene. "The Garvey Movement: A Study in Collective Behavior." Unpublished Master's Thesis, State University of Iowa, 1931.

The writer states that the Garvey Movement was the most significant expression of a nationalistic sentiment yet manifested among American Negroes. The widespread appeal among the masses of the group was both an indication and a cause of a developing race-consciousness heretofore lacking. This development can be understood only as the product of a conflict situation. Discrimination and repression are operating to strengthen the solidarity of the group. The author concludes that the continued growth of a Negro nationalistic spiritism America is probably inevitable. From it, problems are developing which will challenge the best efforts of both races for a solution.

8

CONSTITUTION AND BOOK OF LAWS OF THE UNIVERSAL NEGRO IMPROVEMENT ASSOCIATION AND AFRICAN COMMUNITIES' LEAGUE

Made for the Government of the

Universal Negro Improvement Association,

Inc., and African Communities' League, Inc.,

of the World.

In Effect July, 1918

Revised and Amended August, 1920;

Revised and Amended August, 1921;

Revised and Amended August, 1922

New York, July, 1918

Universal Press, Department of Labor and Industry

56 West 135th Street, New York City, NY

PREAMBLE

The Universal Negro Improvement Association and African Communities' League is a social, friendly, humanitarian, charitable, educational, institutional, constructive, and expansive society, and is founded by persons desiring to the utmost to work for the general uplift of the Negro peoples of the world. And the members pledge themselves to do all in their power to conserve the rights of their noble race and to respect the rights of all mankind, believing always in the Brotherhood of Man and the Fatherhood of God. The motto of the organization is "One God! One Aim! One Destiny!" Therefore, let justice be done to all mankind, realizing that if the strong oppresses the weak, confusion and discontent will ever mark the path of man, but with love, faith, and charity towards all the reign of peace and plenty will be heralded into the world and the generations of men shall be called Blessed.

CONSTITUTION

ARTICLE I

Jurisdiction

Section 1. This body shall be known as the Universal Negro Improvement Assocation and African Communities' League. Its jurisdiction shall include all communities where the people of Negro blood and African descent are to be found. In it alone, and through the Potentate and Supreme Commissioner, hereinafter spoken of, and his successors, are vested powers to establish subordinate divisions and other organizations, whose objects shall coalesce and be identical with those herein set forth, and its mandates shall be obeyed at all times and under all circumstances. To the Universal Negro Improvement Association and African Communities' League, through the authority of the Potentate, is reserved the right to fix, regulate and determine all matters of a general or international nature as affecting the objects of the organization and the membership at large.

Right to Reorganize Rebellious Branch or Division.

Section 2. The right is reserved to revoke charters and to reestablish jurisdiction over any division or subordinate organization whose affairs are conducted contrary to the welfare of the Universal Negro Improvement Association and African Communities' League as required by the Constitution and General Laws.

Objects and Aims

Section 3. The objects of the Universal Negro Improvement Association and African Communities' League shall be: to establish a Universal Confraternity among the race; to promote the spirit of pride and love; to reclaim the fallen; to administer to and assist the needy; to assist in civilizing the backward tribes of Africa; to assist in the development of Independent Negro Nations and Communities; to establish Commissionaries or Agencies in the principal countries and cities of the world for the representation and protection of all Negroes, irrespective of nationality; to promote a conscientious Spiritual worship among the native tribes of Africa; to establish Universities, Colleges, Academies and Schools for the racial education and culture of the people; to conduct a worldwide Commercial and Industrial Intercourse for the good of the people; to work for better conditions in all Negro communities.

Seven Necessary Number for Charter

Section 4. A charter may be issued to seven or more citizens of any community whose intelligence is such as to bring them within respectful recognition of the educated and cultured of such a community, provided there is no chartered division in such a community.

Chapters

Section 5. All additional Divisions created in the same cities shall be called Chapters. The Charters granted to such Divisions shall be called Chapter Charters, and all new Divisions so created shall be called Chapters instead of Divisions, and the Executive Secretary, who shall be a civil servant attached to the Division, shall be the Supervisor of such Chapters.

Dominion, Provincial or Colonial Charters

Section 6. In countries requiring the Provincial or Colonial registration of Charters, there shall be issued one Dominion, Provincial or Colonial Charter, as the law may require, and all Divisions within the Charter limits shall be designated as Branches. Nothing in this provision shall be construed as giving the original Division jurisdiction over the others other than the parent body.

ARTICLE II

Laws

Section 1. The Universal Negro Improvement Association and African Communities' League may enact and enforce laws for its government and that for subordinate divisions, organizations and societies and members throughout the jurisdiction.

Section 2. The laws of the Universal Negro Improvement Association and African Communities League shall be comprised of (a) The Constitution which shall contain the outlines, fundamental principles and policies of the organization, its Jurisdiction and that of local divisions and societies, the list of officers and all matters pertaining to their duties; (b) the By-Laws, which shall contain the order of procedure in Convention, the specific duties of officers and committees, and the standing rules; (c) The Generaal Laws, which shall contain all matters pertaining to the relations of members and local Divisions and societies to each other.

Amendment to Constitution

Section 3. The Constitution shall be amended at times when such amendment tends absolutely to the further interest of the Universal Negro Improvement Association and African Communities' League and when carried by a two-thirds majority in Convention fully assembled.

By-Laws and General Laws: How Enacted

Section 4. By-Laws and General Laws may be enacted by the Convention of the Universal Negro Improvement Association and African Communities' League, and such laws shall be carried by a two-thirds majority.

ARTICLE III

Deputies to Convention

Section 1. Divisions and all kindred organizations, societies and orders subordinate to the Universal Negro Improvement Association and African Communities' League are entitled to representation in Convention; such Divisions and societies sending a delegate or delegates who shall be named deputies, as directed through the office of the President-General.

Terms of Deputies

Section 2. Each Deputy shall hold office for four years after election, and his office shall be honary with its expenses paid for attending Convention by his own Division, organization, society or order. He shall be entitled to one vote in Convention and no proxy shall be allowed.

ARTICLE IV

Officials, Officers, Elections and Appointments

Section 1. The rulers of the Universal Negro Improvement Association and African Communities' League shall be a Potentate and Supreme Commissioner, a Supreme Deputy, a President General, Second Assistant President-General, who shall also be titular Leader of American Negroes; Third Assistant President-General who shall also be titular Leader of the West Indies, South and Central America; a Fourth Assistant General, a Secretary-General, a First Assistant Secretary General, a Second Assistant Secretary General, and a High Chancellor; a Counsel General, an Assistant Counsel-General, Auditor-General; a Minister of Labor and Industry, High Commissioner-General, a Chaplain General, an International Organizer, a Minister of Legions and a Minister of Education, all of whom shall for the High Executive Council representing branches throughout the world, and to or in conflict with the above section, be and is hereby repealed and declared null and void.

Section 2. The offices of the Provisional President of Africa, the President-General and Administrator, the First Assistant President-General, the Second Assistant President-General, who shall also be titular Leader of American Negroes· the Third Assistant President-General, who shall also be titular Leader of Negroes of the West Indies, South and Central America; the Fourth Assistant President-General, all of whom shall be elected and their term of office shall be four years, provided their conduct conforms to the best interests of the Universal Negro Improvement Association and African Communities' League.

Section 2a. All other officers forming the High Executive Council shall be appointed by the President-General and confirmed by the Convention, except the Potentate and the Supreme Deputy, whose terms of office shall be permanent, and such appointments shall be for the same period as that of the Administration, providing their conduct conforms to the best interests of the Universal Negro Improvement Association, and have proven their confidence to the satisfaction of the administration, and

Be it resolved, That everything in the Constitution contradictory to or in conflict with the above section be and is hereby repealed and declared null and void.

Failure of Official to Qualify

Section 3. No person elected to a high office of the Universal Negro Improvement Association shall hold office until his credentials as to his character and qualifications have satisfied the High Executive Council. In case a person elected to a high office is rejected by the High Executive Council, the President-General and Administrator shall have the power to appoint a person to fill the position of the person rejected until the next session of the Convention.

High Commissioners and Commissioners

Section 4. A High Commissioner or Commissioner shall be appointed to represent the Universal Negro Improvement Association in every country where Negroes live. In parts where the country is divided up into large states and different sections a Commissioner shall be appointed to every state and section.

Rank of Minister or Ambassador

Section 5. There shall also be appointed High Commissioners who shall be given the rank of Ministers Plenipotentiary or Ambassadors, who shall be domiciled at the capitals of all regular governments. Their duties shall be to keep up friendly relations with the respective governments and to protect the interests of all Negroes.

Appointment of High Commissioners

Section 6. The Potentate and Supreme Commissioner shall appoint High Commissioners on recommendation of the President General and/Administrator and commission them to represent the interests of the organization in all countries of the world, and they shall be controlled by the office of the High Commissioners-General.

Term of Office of Rulers

Section 8. The term of office of the Potentate and Supreme Commissioner and that of the Supreme Deputy shall be permanent. The term of all other officers of the parent body shall be four years, provided that their conduct conforms with the interests of the Universal Negro Improvement Association and African Communities' League at all times.

ARTICLE V

Potentate and Supreme Commissioner

Section 1. The Potentate and Supreme Commissioner shall be the invested ruler of the Universal Negro Improvement Association and African Communities' League and all its appendages. He shall be of Negro blood and race. He shall constitutionally control all affairs of the Association and League and all societies. He shall institute social orders and societies and organizations in connection with the Universal Negro Improvement Association and African Communities League, as determined by the said Associations and League, and shall retain full power and control over their actions and jurisdiction. He shall have constitutional authority, through his high office, to suspend, reduce or relieve any officer other than the Supreme Deputy of his commission or authority of service to the Universal Negro Improvement Association and African Communities' League and subordinate orders, societies and organizations. He shall issue "articles" or "messages" from time to time to the entire body of members of the Universal Negro Improvement Association and African Communities' League on questions of moment, and such "articles" and "messages" shall be respected by all those claiming allegiance to the Association and League. He shall appear in person to open the Convention and to deliver a speech which shall be a review of the work and operations of the Association and League for the past year, as also advices for the conduct of affairs for the current or following year. He shall make his official residence at the place provided for him by the Universal Negro Improvement Association and African Communities' League. He shall marry only a lady of Negro blood and parentage, and his consort shall herself by virtue of her position be head of the family division of all organizations, societies and orders. He shall form an Executive Council to assist him in his administration and African Communities' League and other elected by the Convention and his colleagues shall be required to be loyal to him and to the Association and League.

He shall be empowered to confer titles, honors, orders of merit, degrees, or marks of distinction on any person or persons who shall have rendered faithful service to the purposes of the Universal Negro Improvement Association and the African Communities' League of whom he has been advised as being fit to bear such titles, honors, orders of merit, degrees or marks of distinction. He shall appoint or commission, through his office, any member of members to carry out any work in the interest of the Association and League. He shall be privileged to nominate his successor during his lifetime, and that nomination shall be handed in a sealed envelope to the High Chancellor, who shall preserve the same until the time of his death. At the time of his death his nomination shall be handed over to the Executive Council, and the Executive Council shall make two other nominations before breaking the seal of the late Potentate's nomination; the nominations of the Executive Council shall be from among officials, officers or distinguished members of the organization who have heretofore distinguished themselves in service to the Universal Negro Improvement Association and African Communities' League and whose honor, loyalty, and devotion cannot be questioned. After breaking the seal of the Potentate's nomination the three nominations shall be announced to the world, and the Supreme Deputy shall call an immediate session of the Convention and then and there elect the new Potentate from the three nominees by majority vote and ballot. The election of a new Potentate from the three nominees shall take place two months after the demise of the former, and his investiture shall take place one month after his election. On the death of the Potentate, and on the election of another, his consort shall vacate the official residence for another to be provided by the Universal Negro Improvement Association and African Communities' League, which shall support her until her death or marriage to another party.

Potentate's Power Derived from Executive Council

Section 2. The Potentate's power of action in all matters shall be derived from the advice received from his Executive Council and through the officers of the Universal Negro Improvement Association and African Communities' League, which advice shall be expressive of the will and sentiment of the people, and he shall not be empowered to act any matter of great moment without first receiving the advice of the Executive Council.

Court Reception or At Home

Section 3. Immediately during the sitting of Convention of each year the Potentate and Supreme Commissioner shall cause to be given at his official residence or at some place of high moral and social repute an "at home" or "reception" which shall be called the "Court Reception" at which the Potentate and his Consort shall receive in presentation those distinguished ladies and gentlemen of the race and their male and female children whose character, morally and socially, stands above question in their respective communities. No lady below the age of eighteen shall be presented at the "Court Reception" and no gentleman below the age of twenty-one. No one shall be received by the Potentate and his Consort who has been convicted of crime or felony, except such crime or felony was committed in the interests of the Universal Negro Improvement Association and African Communities' League, or whose morality is not up to the standard of social ethics. No one shall pay money to be presented at Court, and no one shall be presented at Court who is not known to the President or General Secretary, respectively, of the local Division to which he or she belongs. All recommendations for social recognition shall be made through local Divisions to the office of the High Commissioner-General, who shall edit a list of "social eligibles" and present said list to the Potentate, who shall cause commands from his household to be issued to the respective parties to attend "Court Reception." Recognition for social or other distinctions shall only be merited by previous service to the Universal Negro Improvement Association and African Communities' League by the person or persons to be honored, and no local Division shall recommend anyone to be honored by the Potentate, who has never done some praiseworthy or meritorious service to the organization in the carrying through of its objects, and all persons honored by the Potentate shall be so respected by all Negroes of all countries and climes.

Impeachment of Potentate or Supreme Deputy

Section 4. The Potentate and Supreme Deputy, should they at any time act contrary to the good and welfare of the Universal Negro Improvement Association and African Communitics' League in refusing or neglecting to abide by or carry out the commands of the Association and League through its Constitution and through the order of its Convention shall, on proper evidence of the fact, be impeached by any member of the Executive Council through the office of the Council-General, and they shall be tried for such irregularities, neglect, misconduct or disloyalty to the Association before the Convention, and if found guilty before the Convention shall take immediate steps to elect a new Potentate or Supreme Deputy.

Counsel-General Must Prosecute

Section 5. If the Potentate and Supreme Commissioner or the Supreme Deputy shall be charged or impeached before the Convention, the Counsel-General shall prosecute them in the interest of the Universal Negro Improvement Association and African Communities' League, and the Potentate or Supreme Deputy shall have counsel to appear at the Bar of the Convention in his behalf, and such counsel shall be an active member of or officer of the Universal Negro Improvement Association and African Communities League.

Defendant's Counsel

Section 6. No counsel except an Officer or Active Member of the Universal Negro Improvement Association and African Communities' League shall be allowed to appear in behalf of any member charged before any "responsible body of trial" of the Association and League.

Bribes

Section 7. Should the Potentate and Supreme Commissioner or Supreme Deputy take or receive moneys or gifts from any person or persons by way of bribes or rewards for neglecting or selling out the interests of the Universal Negro Improvement Association and African Communities' League, he shall be guilty of high crime against the Association and League and on conviction before the Convention shall forthwith be disgraced and dismissed from the high office he holds.

Officials Found Guilty

Section 8. Any officer or official of the Universal Negro Improvement Association and African Communities' League charged and found guilty of a similar offense shall be forthwith dismissed from the office of the Association and League through the office of the Potentate or his or her Superior Officer, on the approval of the Executive Council.

Shall Not Receive Money or Gifts

Section 9. No officer or official in the service of the Universal Negro Improvement Association and African Communities' League shall receive money or gifts on his or her account from anyone for services rendered for the Universal Negro Improvement Association and African Communities' League, but all such money and gifts shall be turned over to and shall be the property of the Universal Negro Improvement Association and African Communities' League; but a purse or testimonial may be presented publicly to any officer or official on his or her own account as appreciation of faithful services performed for the Association and League.

All Active Members Must Approve Constitution

Section 10. All officers, officials and active members of the Universal Negro Improvement Association and African Communities' League shall sign their names in approval and acceptance of the Constitution and By-Laws in a register provided for that purpose before they are installed.

ARTICLE VI

Black Star Line Navigation and Trading Company

Section 11. The Third International Convention of Negroes duly assembled ordains and establishes the Black Star Line Navigation and Trading Company, for the purpose of carrying out the steamship program of the Universal Negro Improvement Association in the interests of the race. The Universal Negro Improvement Association shall capitalize the new company and no individuals shall be allowed to own any stock in said Company. All stocks shall be owned absolutely and exclusively by the Universal Negro Improvement Association.

Section 11a. The Executive Council of the Universal Negro Improvement Association is empowered by this Convention to invest its accumulated funds in the said new Steamship Corporation. And the said Executive Council shall be the incorporators of the new Company, and in the formation of the new Company aside from the President-General, no other directors of the defunct Black Star Line Company, shall be allowed to direct the affairs of the new Company. And that only competent persons be employed by the new Company.

Black Star Line Redemption Corporation

Section 12. The Universal Negro Improvement Association in Convention assembled dies hereby authorize the Organization of an auxiliary to be known as the Black Star Line Redemption Corporation, for the purpose of redeeming the stocks and notes of the Black Star Line, Inc., now held by stockholders.

Section 12a. A period of five years shall be allowed for the complete redemption of the stocks and notes of the Black Star Lines, Inc. now held by stockholders and two and one-half percent shall be paid on the stocks and notes to the stockholders from the time of the purchase of said stocks and notes to the time of their redemption.

Section 12b. The Universal Negro Improvement Association is hereby authorized to call upon its Divisions and Chapters throughout the world to give an entertainment once per month to raise funds for the purpose of liquidating the stocks and notes of the stockholders of the Black Star Lines, Inc., and the funds shall be remitted to the Parent Body for the purpose and intent so designed. The Parent Body is further authorized to print and distribute among its Divisions and Chapters envelopes, which shall be used by said Divisions and Chapters in soliciting twenty-five cents from all persons who frequent said entertainments and the amounts collected, together with said envelopes, shall be immediately mailed to the Parent Body, and the funds so received shall be applied to the use for which they were collected.

Supreme Deputy

Section 13. The Supreme Deputy shall assist the Potentate in the discharge of his duties and shall perform the duties of the Potentate in his absence, incapacity or interregnum. He shall be the Potentate's envoy to attend any function or ceremony that the Potentate may be unable to attend himself. He shall attend along with the Potentate the opening of the Convention and sit next to the Potentate. He shall be of Negro blood and parentage.

President-General and Administrator

Section 14. The President-General and Administrator shall be the working head of the Universal Negro Improvement Association and African Communities League and he shall be held responsible to the Potentate for the entire working and carrying out of all commands. He shall attend the Convention and make a speech in reply to that of the Potentate. He shall instruct minor officers on their duties and see that such duties are properly performed.

He shall be empowered to exercise a Veto Power on any financial matter initiated by any individual or by the Executive Council that may tend to jeopardize or ruin the finances of the organization. Such veto power shall only be used by the Administrator in financial matters and were from his best judgment he is convinced that it is not to the best interest of the organization to permit the carrying out of such financial measures. An appeal may be made to the Convention against the veto of the Adminstrator, on any measure, and he shall be responsible to the Convention for the exercise of his judgment on the matter.

First Assistant President-General

Section 15. The First Assistant President-General shall assist the President General in the performance of such duties of his office as shall be assigned to him by the President-General. He shall perform all the duties of the President-General in case of absence, illness, permanent disability, resignation or death, until such time as the Convention shall have elected a new President-General.

Secretary General and High Commissioner

Section 16. The Secretary General and High Commissioner shall have in his custody all correspondence of the Universal Negro Improvement Association and African Communities' League. He shall have under control all Divisional Secretaries and shall conduct the general correspondences of the organization. He shall attend Convention and read reports and answer questions relative to the work of the organization. He shall be the spokesman of the Potentate and Executive Council in Convention.

The Assistant Secretary General

Section 17. The Assistant Secretary General shall assist the Secretary in the performance of such duties of his office as shall be assigned to him by the Secretary General with the approval of the Executive Council and in the event of absence, illness, permanent disability, resignation or death, he shall perform all the duties of the Secretary General until such time as the Convention shall have elected a new Secretary General.

Second Assistant Secretary General

Section 18. It shall be the duty of the Second Assistant Secretary General to work in concert with the First Assistant and the Secretary General in the performance of the duties of that office.

High Chancellor

Section 19. The High Chancellor shall be the custodian of the funds of the Universal Negro Improvement Association and African Communities' League and shall, under the direction of the President General deposit all funds in some responsible bank. He shall give bond to the President General, which bond shall be well recognized. He shall attend Convention and deliver the Financial Speech of the year.

Counsel General

Section 20. The Counsel General shall be the head legal officer of the Universal Negro Improvement Association and African Communities' League. He shall instruct all officials and officers of the Association on the law and shall conduct all cases or see to the defending of the Society before all courts of justice and appear on the Society's behalf at all times as directed by the President General.

Assistant Counsel General

Section 21. The Assistant Counsel General shall asssist the Counsel General in the performance of such duties of his office as shall be assigned to him by the Counsel General with the approval of the Executive Council and in the event of absence, illness, permanent disability, resignation or death he shall perform all the duties of the Counsel General until such time as the Convention shall have elected a new Counsel General.

Auditor General

Section 22. The Auditor General and High Commissioner shall audit the accounts and books of the High Chancellor, and all accounts and books of other high officers and branches twice annually, viz: For the six months ending January 31st within 21 days after that date, and for the six months ending January 31st within 21 days after that date. He shall secure the assistance for this purpose of an expert accountant, and shall submit his report to the President General, who shall cause same to be published in the journal of the Association.

High Commissioner General

Section 23. The High Commissioner General shall be the head of the foreign High Commissioners. He shall receive their reports and report same to the Potentate and Executive Council through the proper officers. He shall recommend to the Potentate worthy individuals on whom commissions, titles, honors, social distinctions and degrees should be conferred.

Chaplain General

Section 24. The Chaplain General shall be the spiritual adviser of the Potentate and Council. He shall act as the representative of the Universal Negro Improvement Association and African Communities' League in conducting the investiture of all high officials and at the conferring of titles, honors, and degrees by the Potentate. He shall attend Convention at its opening along with the Potentate and open the proceedings with prayer.

International Organizer and High Commissioner

Section 25. The International Organizer and High Commissioner shall be charged with the duty of organizing all the Negro communities of the world into the Universal Negro Improvement Association and African Communities' League, and shall have under his control all local organizers, who shall report to him monthly through the officers of their respective local Divisions the results of their various organizing campaigns. He shall make periodic visits to all countries to ascertain and see to the proper bringing together of the world's corporate body of Negroes.

Surgeon General

Section 26. The Surgeon General shall disseminate by lectures, articles and circulars information to the members of our race, with regard to hygiene, eugenics, vital statistics and necessary precautions for the maintenance of health and the increase of life expectation, and shall perform the duties of a physician and surgeon as directed by the President General. He shall publish at least once monthly in the journal of the Association a statement of the physical condition among Negroes. He shall examine the physical fitness of the Officers and Privates of the

Legions and other auxiliaries.

Minister of Labor and Industries

<u>Section 27</u>. The Minister of Labor and Industries shall be an Executive Officer of the Universal Improvement Association, whose duty it shall be to regulate labor and industry of the parent body and among the Divisions and various members of the organization throughout the world. When feasible he should have representatives in each Division, and shall thereby inform himself of the labor conditions throughout the world and formulate plans to relieve the economic conditions of Negroes everywhere. He shall also lend his assistance to all matters of immigration and to the establishment of avenues of industry for the members of the organization.

Minister of Legions

<u>Section 28</u>. The Minister of Legions shall be the Administrative Officer of the Universal African Legions of the Universal Negro Improvement Association. He shall be subjected to the commands of the Potentate, President General and Executive Council. He shall nominate his staff and Chief thereof with the approval of the President General and Potentate, who shall make the actual appointment. He shall use every means, by travel, correspondence and appeal to have a Division of the Legion formed in every city or district. He shall regulate all details as to uniforms, and shall give orders for other movements on the instruction of the President-General or Executive Council. He shall recommend Privates and Officers to the Commander-in-Chief for promotion.

ARTICLE VII

Requirements of Officials and High Officers

<u>Section 1</u>. All officials and high officers of the Universal Negro Improvement Association and African Communities' League shall be Negroes and their consorts or wives shall be Negroes. No one shall be admitted to the high offices of the Association whose life companion is of an alien race.

Qualifications for High and Divisional Officers

<u>Section 2</u>. The qualifications of candidates for high office of the Universal Negro Improvement Association and African Communities' League and for

candidates for divisional offices shall be as follows:

Registered active membership with all dues paid up; shall be a Negro; shall be proven to be conscientious to the cause of racial uplife; he shall not be married to anyone of alien race; shall be free from criminal conviction; shall be of reputable moral standing and good education, and shall undergo a six months' course of instruction at any University of the Universal Negro Improvement Association, and that only when the student graduates that he be allowed to represent the organization; and for a correspondence course of one year shall be established for the same purpose, and this course shall be extended to all persons of the race who desire to take it.

ARTICLE VIII

Salaries and Expenses

Section 1. The salary of the Potentate and Supreme Commissioner shall be in keeping with his high office and responsibilities, which salary shall be granted by the Convention. The Potentate shall labor for the good and welfare of the organization, irrespective of salary or other consideration.

Section 2. The Supreme Deputy shall be subjected to the same conditions on matter of salary as the Potentate.

High Officers

Section 3. All officials and high officers of the Universal Negro Improvement Association and African Communities' League other than the Potentate and Supreme Commissioner and Supreme Deputy shall be granted salaries commensurate with the work they perform, which shall be voted by the Convention.

Salaries of High Officials

Section 3a. All officials of the Universal Negro Improvement Association shall be paid their salaries at the minimum which shall be half of the maximum, and each shall be allowed to earn the maximum by ability and fitness, which maximum shall be paid at the end of each month according to the record of such official.

Salaries of Divisional Officers

Section 4. Officers of local Divisions who

give their entire time to the working of their local Divisions shall receive salaries for their services according to the ruling of the membership of such local Divisions, and all such salaries shall be conditional on the local Division having at its disposal sufficient funds in its treasury to make payment of such possible.

Transfer of Officers

Section 5. The President or any other officer of a local Division in the pay of the Universal Negro Improvement Association and African Communities' League shall be subjected to annual, bi-annual, or triannual transfers, according to the advices of the offices of the President General and Executive Council.

Departmental Assistant

Section 6. No department of the Parent Body shall employ an Assistant for that Department without first obtaining the approval of the President General as to the fitness and desirability of the individual to be employed.

ARTICLE IX

Revenue, Incomes, Etc.

Section 1. The Revenue of the Universal Negro Improvement Association and African Communities' League shall be derived from monthly subscriptions, which shall not be more than twenty-five cents per month, being authorized dues of each active member, donations, collections, gifts, profits derived from businesses, entertainments, functions or general amusements of an innocent nature and a death tax of ten cents per month.

Division Responsible for Tax

That a tax of $1 shall be levied on every member of the UNIA each and every year, payable on the first of January, for the purpose of defraying expenses of the organization and its general upkeep, and said one dollar collected from each member shall be forwarded to the High Chancellor through the office of the Secretary General at headquarters.

Annual Expense Tax

That One Dollar annual tax of each member shall be charged against the local Division to which the member is attached, and shall be collected from the financial membership of the Division as by its report on the 31st of December of each year.

Section 2. The revenue of the Universal Negro Improvement Association and African Communities League shall be apportioned to the General Fund, which shall go to bear the general expenses of the organization for the carrying out of its objects.

Remitting of Monthly Dues by Local Divisions, Societies, Etc.

Section 3. The Secretaries of all Divisions and subordinate organizations shall remit at the end of each month to the High Chancellor, through the Secretary General, one-fifth of all monthly subscriptions, joining fees, dues and net profits from local business under the control of the said Division, as also from donations, grants, gifts, amusement, entertainments and other functions for the general fund of the Universal Negro Improvement Association and African Communities' League for the carrying out of its general objects. That each person pay an entrance fee of twenty-five cents in joining the Association.

Chancellor Deposits All Money

Section 4. All moneys of the Universal Negro Improvement Association and African Communities' League shall be lodged by the Chancellor in a responsible bank, and drawn only on the signatures of the President General, the High Chancellor and Secretary General.

Donations to Charity by Potentates, Etc.

Section 5. The Potentate and Supreme Commissioner shall be empowered to make donations of charity to be created from the Charitable Fund of the Universal Negro Improvement Association and African Communities League, to worthy causes in the name of the Association and League, with the approval of the Executive Council.

Investing of Money

Section 6. The Universal Negro Improvement Association and African Communities League and all its

Divisions and allied societies may invest money in any business which to the best judgment of the members of the organization are of such as to yield profit in the interest of the Association, but no Division shall invest its funds without first getting the approval of the Parent Body.

No Investments by Divisions

Section 7. No investment of money shall be made by a local Division or society without the consent of the membership of the said Division or society with the approval of the Parent Body.

Selling Outside Stock

Section 8. No Division shall allow any of its officers or members to use the meetings of the organization for selling stocks or shares in any personal or private concern, and any such officer or member found guilty of such offense shall be suspended for three months.

Section 9. The Parent Body of the Universal Negro Improvement Association and African Communities' League may invest its money wholly or in company with others for the good of the organization.

Section 10. The funds of the Universal Negro Improvement Association and African Communities' League as derived from all sources herein mentioned shall be used for the carrying out of the objects of the Association.

Net Proceeds to Divisions

Section 11. Fifty percent of the proceeds of all entertainments given by auxiliaries of Divisions, Bran ches or Chapters shall be turned over to the Divisions, Branch or Chapter after all legitimate expenses incurred for such entertainments have been paid, and no auxiliary shall give any entertainment without the permission of the President of the Division, Branch or Chapter.

Section 12. All auxiliaries of Divisions must turn into the treasury of the Divisions to which they are attached all moneys derived from entertainments at the first meeting following such entertainments.

ARTICLE X

Membership

Section 1. All persons of Negro blood and African descent are regarded as ordinary members of the Universal Negro Improvement Association and African Communities' League, and are entitled to the consideration of the organization. Active members are those who pay the monthly dues for the upkeep of the organization, who shall have first claim on the Association for all benefits to be dispensed.

ARTICLE XI

Sitting of Executive Council

Section 1. The Executive Council of the Universal Negro Improvement Association and African Communities' League shall assemble at the headquarters of the Association and shall consist of all the high officers of the Association and others elected thereto. The Potentate shall be its Chairman, and in his absence the President General and Administrator, and the Secretary General its Secretary. It shall decide all questions arising between Divisions and subordinate societies appeals, international questions, and all matters affecting the good and welfare of the organization and its members at large during the rising of the convention.

ARTICLE XII

Auditing Accounts

Section 1. The President General shall cause the books and accounts of the High Chancellor and subordinate officers to be audited twice a year as follows: All accounts for the six months ending July 31st within 15 days after that date, and for the same period ending January 31st, within 15 days after that date. For this purpose he shall call upon the Auditor General and also appoint an expert accountant who shall make a thorough examination and shall submit a report to the President General, who shall cause its publication in the regular journal of the society.

Defalcation or Misappropriation

Section 2. If said report should show any errors

of importance or defalcation or misappropriation of funds of any officers so responsible, it shall be the duty of the President General, with the consent of the Potentate, to suspend any officer of officers, and he shall instruct the Counsel General to proceed at once, legally, to secure the Universal Negro Improvement Association and African Communities' League from loss, and in accordance with the bond or bonds of said officers or officer.

Fiscal Year

Section 3. The fiscal year of the Universal Negro Improvement Association and African Communities' League shall commence on the first day of June and end on the 31st day of May in each year.

ARTICLE XIII

The Civil Service

Section 1. A Civil Service shall be established by the Universal Negro Improvement Association. From this Civil Service shall be recruited all employees of the Association.

Preference of Civil Servants

Section 2. A civil servant shall have precedence over and perference to all persons employed, or to be employed, by the Universal Negro Improvement Association.

Lists

Section 3. An official civil servants' list of the Universal Negro Improvement Association shall be compiled and designated as the Civil Service.

Examination

Section 4. All person to be placed on the Civil Service shall first be obliged to pass an examination on general educational test as laid down by the official examiners, and in addition thereto such persons shall be required to give evidence of good moral character and honesty.

Examiners

Section 5. The official examiners shall be the Administrator of the Universal Negro Improvement Association and such other persons as he may appoint to serve with him.

Civil Service Commission

Section 6. The persons appointed by the Administrator to serve with him as official examiners shall be known as the Civil Service Commission; and the Civil Service Commission, together with the Administrator, shall compose the Board of Civil Service Examiners. They shall designate the subjects in which applicants shall be examined, and shall also prescribe the rules and regulations governing the examinations of applicants.

Certificate

Section 7. All applicants who have passed the Civil Service examination shall be given a certificate as proof thereof.

Promotions

Section 8. All promotions in the Universal Negro Improvement Association shall be made from the Civil Service list of the Association.

Section 9. All Executive Secretaries of local divisions shall be members of the Civil Service.

ARTICLE XV

Passport Identifications

Section 1. A bureau of Passports shall be attached to the Secretary-General's office.

Section 2. Each and every member who desires a Passport Identification for the purpose of travel or for the purpose of receiving recognition, consideration and likely help from other branches, or for the purpose of proving connection with a regular organization or with a branch of the Universal Negro Improvement Association, shall be supplied with one of these Passports at any Division of the organization by the Executive Secretary of that Division at which application is duly made.

Section 3. Each passport shall have on its face a photograph of the bearer, the signature of the bearer and such other details as may be provided in the rules and regulations of the Bureau of Passports and Identifications.

Section 4. Each passport identification shall be issued by the Universal Negro Improvement Association and African Communities' League from its headquarters. It shall be signed and stamped by the Executive Secretary stationed at the Division where the passport has been secured.

Section 5. Before a passport identification can be secured each and every member shall be required to fill out a bill of particulars, and only financial members whose dues and assessments have been fully paid up and whose records are clean shall be granted a passport identification until he or she shall have been in the organization for six months and shall have paid up all dues and assessments.

Section 6. The sum of two dollars shall be paid for the issuance of every Passport Identification. Renewals may be made annually against the payment of a fee of twenty-five cents.

Section 7. The Bureau of Justice, through the office of the President-General, shall see that each and every member who holds a passport identification is properly protected, in case of abuse, advantage or injustice committed upon such individual.

African Redemption Fund

1. The parent body shall be empowered to raise a universal fund from all Negroes for the purpose of the redemption of Africa. Every member of the Negro race shall be asked to contribute to this fund a sum not less than Five Dollars. This contribution to the African Redemption Fund shall not be a tax on active members, but shall be a voluntary contribution by all Negroes.

2. This fund shall be known as the "African Redemption Fund."

3. Each and every person who subscribes to this fund shall receive a certificate of loyalty to the cause "Africa." The certificate shall bear the signatures of the President-General, the High Chancellor and the Secretary-General of the Universal Negro Improvement Association.

4. The purpose of the African Redemption Fund shall be to create a working capital for the organization and to advance the cause for the building up of Africa.

ARTICLE XV

Bureau of Justice

1. A Bureau of Justice shall be established by the parent body of the UNIA and ACL for the protection of all Negroes.

2. The Bureau of Justice shall be composed of three members. It shall have for its head an attorney-at-law who shall be known as the chief of the Bureau of Justice. One of the members of the Bureau shall be its secretary.

3. The Bureau shall have to cooperate with it a committee of three from each Local Division, composed of the President and two members selected from the general membership. This committee shall be under the supervision of the Bureau.

4. The local committee shall have the power to dispose of all matters not of sufficient magnitude to require special attention of the Bureau, and shall report to the Bureau their action therein.

5. The Bureau, with the consent and advice of the President-General and High Executive Council, shall have the power to make such rules and incur such expenses as are absolutely necessary for the proper carrying out of its objects.

RULES AND REGULATIONS FOR UNIVERSAL AFRICAN LEGIONS OF THE UNIA AND ACL

ARTICLE I

(Name and Object)

Section 1. This Auxiliary body shall be known as the Universal African Legions and shall consist of men who are active members of the Universal Negro Improvement Association and African Communties' League, and between the ages of 18 and 55 years and in good health.

Section 2. This Auxiliary body shall have the special designation of the Universal African Legions and shall prepare men for service by teaching them military skill and discipline and by registering them according to the various trades in which they have been trained.

There shall be among them noncommissioned officers and men of three classes, viz: First Class Master Workmen, Second Class Skilled Workmen and Third Class Unskilled Workmen. The Master and Skilled must have trade identifications. Unskilled workmen must be grouped without trade identification.

ARTICLE II

Location

Section 1. The quarters of the Universal African Legions shall be the Liberty Hall or the meeting place of the Division of the UNIA and ACL in which they are formed and unto which they shall be attached.

Section 2. The Headquarters of the Universal African Legions shall be with the Parent Body of the UNIA and ACL and shall be under the direct supervision of the Minister of Legions.

ARTICLE III

Commissioned Officers

Section 1. The Minister of Legions Staff shall consist of Generals, Lieutenant Generals, Major Generals and Commanders, and such other Departmental General Officers that may be expedient for the success ful conduct of the UAL.

Section 2. The Generals, Lieutenants Generals, Major Generals and Commanders shall be appointed by the Minister of Legions with the approval of the President General and Administrator. All Commissioners shall rank as Brigadier Generals and shall be posted as to their duties where the Legion is concerned in their respective fields. The President of each local Division and chapter by virtue of his office shall be the ranking Commander of his Division.

Section 2a. All orders affecting the Universal African Legion issued to Divisions or Chapters shall be issued through the President of the local Division or chapter, who in turn shall issue to the Military Commander of his Division or chapter, all of which shall first be approved by the President General and Administrator.

Section 3. Commissioned Officers of the various Divisions or Brigades when fully organized shall be as follows:

1. Commander-President of the Local Division
2. Colonel
3. Honorary Colonel (inactive, except for consultation or advice)
4. Lieutenant Colonel
5. Majors
6. Captains
7. First Lieutenants
8. Second Lietenants
9. Cadet or Boy Scouts Commander (Second Lieutenant)

Staff Officers' Insignia

General - Sphinx and six buttons
Major General - Sphinx and five buttons
Lieutenant General - Sphinx and four buttons

Commander - Sphinx and three buttons
Inspector General - Sphinx and two buttons

Divisional Officers' Insignia

Colonel - Six buttons
Lieutenant Colonel - Five buttons
Major - Four buttons
Captain - Three buttons
First Lieutenants - Two buttons
Second Lieutenants - One button

ARTICLE IV

Non-Commissioned Officers and Men and Manual of Instruction

Section 1. The Headquarters of the Universal African Legions shall adopt and authorize a uniform system of training and discipline which shall be used by all branches of the Legions wherever domiciled.

ARTICLE V

Quartermaster and Staff

Section 1. There shall be established in the Unit of each Division or Brigade a Quartermaster and Staff, who shall receive moneys, collections and deposits for uniform. They shall make weekly and monthly reports to the Commander through the General Secretary. All moneys received by the Quartermaster shall be lodged with the Treasurer of the Division for deposit in the Bank so designated, as part of the funds of the Division, for which the Legions shall be credited.

Section 2. The Quartermaster shall receive all moneys designated to the Universal African Legions and shall pay all debts with the approval of the Commanders and issue vouchers for same.

ARTICLE VI

Commissariat and Its Duties

Section 1. Each Brigade or Division shall have a Comissary of Subsistence Department which shall be composed in ratio to the size of the Division. The head shall be known as the Commissary Captain and shall function directly under the Commander of the Division.

Section 2. The Commissary Officer of a Division shall be a caterer and have knowledge of feeding and refreshing his Brigade while on the march, camping or other outings. He shall under instructions of the Commander see that refreshments are prepared and served to each unit while outing, camping or hiking and with the assistance of his department ensure equal distribution. In case where special catering by him is unnecessary he shall use his department to supervise those who have volunteered or are paid to do so.

Section 3. When the Brigade is normally at rest at its quarters and the duties of the Commissariat are not necessary, each member of the Commissariat shall muster back to his Division. When needed the Commissary Officers shall apply to the Colonel or Commanding Officer of each unit for the number wanted under orders from the Commander.

Section 4. When more than one Division or Brigade is on the hike or move, the Minister of the Legions shall appoint a Commissary General, who shall supervise all duties of the Commissariat hereinbefore mentioned, with the addition of sleeping and living quarters. Any inconvenience of living, sleeping or feeding by any member or unit in a Brigade shall be communicated through the Commissary Officer in Command to the Commissary General.

ARTICLE VII

Yearly Tax and Other Expenses

Section 1. Each member of this Auxiliary shall pay on the first day of January, each year, the sum of twenty-five cents into the fund of the Universal African Legion. The Quartermaster of each Division shall receive the tax, issue proper vouchers and turn over the money to the Secretary of the Division who shall forward it to Headquarters in conjunction with the general report of the Parent Body.

Section 2. Every Division of Brigade shall bear the expenses of the Staff Officer who shall be sent from Headquarters at the invitation of said Division or Brigade to visit the whole or any unit thereof.

Section 3. Any Division or Brigade may make a weekly collection from its members to finance the working thereof; such collection not to exceed ten cents weekly for non-commissioned officers and men. Such collections have nothing whatsoever to do with the yearly Tax for Headquarters, neither shall it be regarded as Dues of the local Division.

ARTICLE VIII

Examinations for Office

Section 1. Any officer before receiving his commission shall be required to pass an examination by an Examining Board named by the Minister of Legions.

The subjects shall be chosen from the following:

Geography of Africa	Writing
Languages	Mathematics
Topography	Reading

Signalling including Morse. Semaphore Telegraphy.

And any other subjects that are necessary for the fullfillment of the duties assigned to the position for which he applies.

Each officer shall be required to obtain 75 percent marks for graduation in his ability test. Each officer shall also bring with his application 75 percent marks for good conduct, i.e., 75 out a 100 ability and 75 out of a 100 good conduct.

ARTICLE IX

Disciplinary Powers of Officers in Command

Section 1. Under these regulations as ratified by the Second International Convention of the UNIA and ACL and which shall be from time to time amended by succeeding Conventions, the Commanding Officer of any attachment, company or high command may, for minor offenses not denied by the accused, impose disciplinary punishments upon persons of his command without the intervention of a court martial, unless the accused demands trial by court martial.

Section 2. The disciplinary punishments authorized by this Article shall include admonition, reprimand, withholding of privileges, extra fatigue and restriction to certain specified limits, but shall not include fines or confinements under guard.

ARTICLE XXV

Oath

All members shall be required before receiving cards of commissions to take the following vow. This vow shall be printed in small type at the back of their cards or at the bottom of their commissions.

The vow to be taken by all members of the Universal Negro Improvement Association and African Communities' League shall be as follows:

> I - - - in the presence of the Supreme God of the Universe and all persons here assembled, do solemnly vow, that I do here and now dedicate my whole life to the Universal Negro Improvement Association and African Communities' League and the cause of the redemption of my Motherland, Africa.
>
> That I pledge strict obedience and support to His Highness the Potentate and all other persons designated by him or representing him.
>
> That I shall never disgrace myself or my uniform by insubordination or contemptuous behavior of any kind.
>
> That I shall discreetly and to the best of my ability spiritually, mentally and physically defend the cause of the UNIA and ACL from all enemies within and without, and also do my utmost to build up and protect the morale of its members to the end that God's Divine purpose be speedily accomplished in the ultimate freedom of all mankind from slavery and despoilation and particularly the cause of the Redemption of Africa.

RULES AND REGULATIONS GOVERNING THE UNIVERSAL AFRICAN BLACK CROSS NURSES

ARTICLE I

Name

This auxiliary of the Universal Negro Improvement Association shall be named the Universal African Black Cross Nurses.

ARTICLE II

Section 1. The objects of this auxiliary shall be to carry on a system of relief and to supply the same in mitigating the suffering caused by pestilence, famine, fire, floods and other great calamities, and to devise and carry on measures for preventing same.

Section 2. To attend to the sick of the Division to which the public auxiliary is attached and be ready for service at any time when called upon by His Highness the Potentate.

Section 3. To issue pamphlets which will tend to educate the public to the use of safety devices and prevention of accident; to instruct in sanitation for prevention of epidemics; and to instruct in First Aid.

ARTICLE III

Membership

Section 1. All women of Negro blood and African descent between the ages of 16 and 45 may become members of this auxiliary.

Section 2. Only active members of the Universal Negro Improvement Association shall be admitted to membership in this auxiliary.

Section 3. All women of the Race not desiring active membership may become Honorary Members upon payment of One Dollar or more annually.

Section 4. All men of the race shall be permitted to become Honorary members of this auxiliary upon payment of One Dollar or more annually.

Section 5. All honorary members shall be known as annual or sustaining members.

RULES AND REGULATIONS GOVERNING THE UNIVERSAL AFRICAN MOTOR CORPS

ARTICLE I

Name

This auxiliary of the Universal Negro Improvement Association shall be named the Universal African Motor Corps.

ARTICLE II

The object of this auxiliary shall be to assist the Universal African Legions in the performance of their duties.

ARTICLE III

Section 1. All active members of the Universal Negro Improvement Association between the ages of 16 and 45 may become members of this auxiliary. The male membership shall, however, be confined to only those who are in active command of the units of the various divisions. All commissioned Officers above the rank of Major shall automatically be Officers of this auxiliary.

Section 2. This auxiliary shall be trained in "Military Discipline" by the Officers of the Universal African Legions. They shall also be given such automobile instructions as driving, repairs, etc.

ARTICLE IV

Management

Section 1. The Universal Head of the Motor Corps shall be a Brigadier-General, who shall be a lady. She shall be fairly educated and shall be a trained and licensed Chauffeur. She shall be attached to the office of the Minister of Legions.

Section 2. The local Officers of this auxiliary shall be a Captain, a first and second Lieutenant and such non-commissioned officers as may be found necessary. The Captain shall be the President of the Unit and the First and Second Lieutenants shall be its Secretary and Treasurer respectively.

Section 3. All divisional staff officers, meaning Commander and active head of each Unit of the Universal African Legion shall be ranking officers of this auxiliary.

RULES AND REGULATIONS FOR JUVENILES

ARTICLE I

Infant Class: One Year to Seven Years

Subjects:

Bible Class and Prayer, Doctrine of the UNIA and ACL. Facts about the Black Star Steamship Corporation, The Negro Factories Corporation and History of Africa (in story book fashion).

Class Two or Girl's Souvenir Class: (Age 7 - 13 years).

Subjects:

Taught to make Souvenirs with cloth, needle and thread, for sale for Juvenile Department, Ritual of UNIA, Write Negro Stories, taught Race pride and love, Taught Negro History and Etiquette and be given disciplinary training by the Legions.

Class Two or Boy's Souvenir Class: (Age 7 - 13 years).

Subjects:

Will be given same training as girls of Number Two Class, the only difference being that the boys of this class shall make souvenirs with wood and carved instead of with needle.

UNIA and ACL Cadets (Age 13 - 16 Years). Training:

Ritual of UNIA; Military Training; Flag signaling; Negro History. (Books advised) "From Superman to Man," "White Capital and Colored Labor," "When Africa Awakes," "African Lore and Lyrics." This class must be taught by a member of the Legions who is acquainted with military tactics.

RULES FOR THE UNIVERSAL IMPROVEMENT ASSOCIATION CHOIRS

ARTICLE I

Names and Objects

Section 1. This auxiliary shall be known as the Universal Negro Association Choir. It shall consist of men and women who are active members of the Universal Negro Improvement Association and African Communities' League.

Section 2. Its object shall be to furnish vocal talent in the form of solos, duets, trios, quartettes, quintettes, choruses, etc., for the various meetings and services held by the organization as may be expedient.

ARTICLE II

Officers and Their Duties

Section 1. The officers shall be a President, Secretary-Librarian, a Treasurer and a Musical Instructor, who shall not be President.

Section 2. Besides the foregoing officers mentioned in Section 1 of this Article, there shall be a leading soprano, a mezzo soprano, leading alto, a first tenor, and basso profundo and a pianist and assistant instructor.

Section 3. The duties of the musical instructor shall be to instruct the choir in music.

Section 4. The duties of the President shall be to supervise at all meetings, rehearsals, services and other functions, and manage all affairs pertaining to the choir and its obligations to the organization.

Section 5. The duties of the Secretary-Librarian are to keep a record of the members of the choir, their attendance to rehearsals, services, etc. for the information of the President of the division. He shall write all notices, attend to the general correspondence and keep a record of the properties of the choir.

Index

Including authors, joint authors, and editors.
Numbers refer to individual entry numbers.

ABOUT THE COMPILERS

Lenwood G. Davis is Assistant Professor of History at Winston-Salem State University in North Carolina. His books include *I Have a Dream: The Life and Times of Martin Luther King, Jr.* (Greenwood Press, 1973), *Black Women in America, The Black Family in the United States* (with Janet L. Sims, Greenwood Press, 1978), *Black Artists in the United States* (with Janet L. Sims, Greenwood Press, 1980), and *The Black Aged in the United States* (forthcoming, Greenwood Press).

Janet L. Sims is Reference Librarian at the Moorland-Spingarn Research Center of Howard University in Washington, D.C. In addition to assisting Dr. Davis with *The Black Family in the United States* and *Black Artists in the United States*, she compiled the bibliography of *Black Women in the Employment Sector*. She is the author of *The Progress of Afro-American Women* (Greenwood Press, 1980) and *Marian Anderson: An Annotated Bibliography and Discography* (forthcoming, Greenwood Press).